THE
BACK PAGE

Byron Crawford's Kentucky Living *Columns*

ILLUSTRATIONS BY PHILIP HARRIS

Kentucky Electric Cooperatives, Louisville, Kentucky

First Printing August 2023

ISBN: 978-1-953058-86-7
Library of Congress Control Number: 2023941453

Cover photo: Eric Crawford
Design: Katy Hurt
Editor: Shannon Brock
Managing editor: Joel Sams
Copy editor: Madelynn Coldiron

Printed in the United States of America

Published by Kentucky Electric Cooperatives
P.O. Box 32170
Louisville, KY 40232

Distributed by Butler Books
www.butlerbooks.com
info@butlerbooks.com

To our children, Eric, Andrea, Joe and Wes, and to the memory of their mother, my late wife, Jackie, who is missed more than she will ever know.

CONTENTS

FOREWORD

Sometimes a story pieces together so well, we'll say, "You couldn't have made it up." The great storytellers of our time, Byron Crawford included, recount reality so beautifully—and the twists and turns are so coincidental—that fiction couldn't compare.

As a community journalist in the late 2000s, I visited classrooms and talked to children about my job: What did I do? How did I get there? I would tell them the answer to those questions began in high school. When considering my career options, I took a deep dive into things I already liked to do and one of them stood out: I loved to read magazines.

"But," I would tell the classes, "for whatever reason, I don't read them front to back. Instead, I'll open them, back page first, and read from back to front."

Fast forward 10 years, and I found myself as managing editor of *Kentucky Living*, visiting electric cooperatives across the state. As I talked with consumer-members, often among the first things they would say was, "I love your magazine. That back page column—it's so good, that's what I flip to first."

With *Kentucky Living*, we don't have to guess the reason our readers are going to the back page. We know it's because of Byron—because of his incredible skill set, because of his voice, because he can tell you a story about a safety pin and make you cry.

Byron began writing Byron Crawford's Kentucky in January 2011 after longtime columnist David Dick passed away. You'll read Byron's reflections on that in just a few pages—and, not to spoil anything—but Byron recalls David's humility. Maybe that's an inherent characteristic of a good storyteller, because Byron Crawford is one of the humblest people you'll ever meet. Though it carries his name, his monthly column isn't about him—it is about the stories he tells. Even when the stories are about his own upbringing and memories, the tales become the characters and take on a life of their own.

Kentucky Living is the most widely circulated print publication in the state and is published by Kentucky Electric Cooperatives, the statewide association that supports 26 electric cooperatives in Kentucky. Our two generation and transmission cooperatives and 24 distribution cooperatives have consumer-members in 117 of 120 counties.

As a statewide association, it's our job to support those cooperatives, much in the way that the cooperatives support their members. And it's those members whose stories are being told in our magazine, including in the columns that follow these pages.

I became editor of *Kentucky Living* in 2023, the same year our team embarked upon compiling and publishing this book. Somehow, a small-town Kentucky girl who wanted to work for a magazine because she liked to read them back to front has realized that dream and is a part of a book titled *The Back Page*. It's almost so perfect, I couldn't have made it up.

Editing Byron's columns, working with him monthly and now collaborating on this book have provided a series of "pinch-me" moments in my life. I'm honored and proud to be a part of it all.

Readers of *Kentucky Living* have known and loved Byron Crawford's stories for more than 12 years, so we know you'll love, laugh and cry with this collection. But don't start at the back page on this one. There are too many true tales you wouldn't want to miss.

—Shannon Brock
Editor, *Kentucky Living*
June 2023

PROLOGUE

The Beginning

JANUARY 2011

Following in giant footprints

As I write these first few lines on the back page of *Kentucky Living*—the home of David Dick's wonderful columns for the past 21 years—an old déjà vu returns.

Throughout my career in broadcast and print journalism, it has been both my good fortune and curse to have followed legendary personalities in nearly every assignment.

Here I go again.

In the years I knew David, I would have assumed that because we were about the same height and build, we might have worn nearly the same size shoes. Yet suddenly, his old shoes look way too big for me.

I remember the same feeling when I began writing the "Kentucky Column" for *The Courier Journal* in Louisville 31 years ago, following in the giant ink footprints left by the beloved Allan Trout and Joe Creason. And again, when I took a seat behind the microphones at WHAS radio and television for the first time to deliver newscasts that once were voiced by the likes of Pete French, Paul Clark and, yes, David Dick before he was hired by CBS News.

Not only had I been a friend of David's since his return to Kentucky from CBS, but I was always admiring of his work and was especially touched by his gentle spirit and uncommon modesty.

Lexington Herald-Leader columnist Paul Prather wrote a moving tribute to David a few weeks after his funeral. "You couldn't make him brag on himself," says Prather, who remembers asking David how he won an Emmy for his network reporting about the attempted assassination of presidential candidate George Wallace in 1972.

Actually, he had a talented film crew who managed to pick up the gunshots fired by the would-be assassin, David said. He'd won the Emmy because of his film crew.

Yep, that's the David Dick I knew.

My hope is that in the months ahead, my words will be worthy of this space that he filled so eloquently for so long with stories about the people, places, and everyday life in this 25.8-million acre socio-geographic jigsaw puzzle called Kentucky.

David and I shared one most essential qualification for this job: a love for Kentucky that's as wide as the Mississippi and as deep as Lake Cumberland.

When David and his wife, Lalie, invited me to pen the foreword for their book *Home Sweet Kentucky* a few years ago, I wrote that when they looked into Kentucky's eyes, they saw clear through to her soul.

With your help and with grace from the Almighty, my hope is to continue looking into those eyes and sharing with you many more Kentucky moments worth remembering—if not with David's remarkable gift for words, then certainly with his love for the subject.

Oh friend David, what size are these big shoes you have left me?

Potbellied stoves and liars' benches, page 6

I

Memories

MARCH 2011

Potbellied stoves and liars' benches

A few of them are still around, but sadly, most of Kentucky's rustic country stores have gone the way of the nickel Coke and the 20-cent bologna sandwich.

Many of us who grew up in rural Kentucky during the first three-quarters of the 20th century have fond memories of a country store not far from our house.

Don Carter, who lives on Big Hickman Creek in Jessamine County, was mourning the passing of country stores a few months ago in sentiments bordering on poetic.

The essence of his lament was that country stores were once the cultural hitching posts of most rural communities.

On their porches and around their potbellied stoves and liars' benches, everything was discussed from family problems to politics to farming, to romance and high finance—more often laced with humor than rancor.

Carter remembered a local character known as "Pup" Corman, who had a large family. As Pup left the store one winter afternoon, someone asked, "Pup, why are you leaving so early?"

"I've got to get home and crack enough walnuts to feed 13 children," Pup answered.

At Penn's Store near Gravel Switch, one of Kentucky's oldest country stores, the high water marks from local floods through the decades are still visible on the primitive counter.

At R.C. Weddle's old store in neighboring Casey County, soft drink bottle caps covered the parking lot, and Weddle's regular customers all knew that if a stick of firewood was propped against the screen door, it meant the store was closed.

The community of Tolu in Crittenden County is said to have taken its name from a whiskey-based tonic made from a Colombian tolu tree extract that was served at a country store in the settlement during Prohibition.

During the 1950s, there were more than 1,000 country stores nestled among the hollows and crossroads of southeastern and southern Kentucky where the Laurel Grocery Company delivered its wholesale orders.

Don Chesnut of London, whose father, W.J. "Bill" Chesnut, co-founded the grocery company along with George Griffin, tells of a country store owner in Clay County who was unable to pay the wholesaler a $60 debt, a sizeable sum in the early 1930s.

Chesnut and Griffin went to collect and found that there was little left to claim as collateral. Then they noticed a cow grazing behind the store and made a deal with the storekeeper to square the debt in exchange for the cow. They promised to send a truck to haul her back to London.

Weeks passed and winter set in, and the truck never made it to get the cow. Then one day in the spring, there came a notice in the mail from the storekeeper that Chesnut and Griffin owed him a feed bill for keeping their cow all winter.

The bill, he said, amounted to about $60. They agreed to settle the debt in exchange for the cow.

JUNE 2011

Souvenir memories

With another vacation season just a suitcase away, I am remembering a story my friend, the late Jodie Hall of Grayson County, often recalled of his family's vacation visit to the Grand Canyon.

As they stood at an overlook on the canyon rim, under the streaming shadow of a large American flag, another family arrived.

They might have been subjects in a Norman Rockwell painting: two parents, young children, and an elderly little woman carrying a large purse and wearing a scarf pulled tight across her head and tied under her chin.

The parents stood for a while, almost spellbound by the view. Then the man turned to the older lady and asked, "Mom, what do you think of it?"

She looked around for a moment, then shot back, "The wind sure is a flappin' that flag, ain't it."

Over the years, I have come to realize that great vacations are not measured so much in destinations and dollars as in souvenir memories of small moments.

Our family visited the Grand Canyon once, but my fondest recollection of that trip is of the night we took a large room in a Best Western motel in Tucumcari, New Mexico. My wife, Jackie, our four children and I slept in the same room.

We laughed more as a family that night than we had in months. It sounded like a half-dozen 10-year-olds at a sleepover—who'd sugared up on ice cream and cupcakes just before bedtime.

Rushing to more tourist stops the next morning, two of the most enduring images I saw from the van window were a grove of quaking aspens shimmering in the sun and a cowboy on horseback moving a herd of cattle on the open range.

John Steinbeck touched a nerve in his early 1960s classic, *Travels with Charley: In Search of America*, when he declared that the interstate highways then being built across the country would make it possible "to drive from New York to California without seeing a single thing."

But for today's highway travelers who take time to look, there is still much to see. Interstates and bypasses have literally cut through the backyards and back pastures of America, and now offer a behind-the-scenes glimpse of a countryside that may have been hidden from Steinbeck and his pet poodle half a century ago.

The novelist could scarcely have dreamed that today it would be video games, DVD players, iPhones, iPads, Nooks, Kindles and an arsenal of other digital distractions that would make the view from the car window virtually obsolete.

Given a few vacations to do over, I would enjoy our children more and worry less about where we were going and what time we'd arrive. Something else Steinbeck said keeps coming back to me:

"We find after years of struggle that we do not take a trip; a trip takes us."

SEPTEMBER 2011

Pride and picture day

With schools open again, it won't be long before "picture day."
You remember that day in school, once a year, when we had our pictures made, then waited to see if they were any good. When they came back, most parents bought a few, and kids exchanged small pictures with classmates.

After Kenneth Croslin of Warren County read my February column urging readers to write their personal stories (page 196), he sent me a few of his stories, including one about his school pictures in 1964, the year he was in ninth grade at Alvaton High School.

He explained that he was the second youngest of 11 children of a sharecropper's family in Warren County. His father, Phillip, died of a heart attack while working in the fields at age 51, and Kenneth's mother, Julia, found a job as an aide in a nursing home, earning 65 cents an hour. Times were tough.

Kenneth got free lunches at school by scraping leftover food from cafeteria plates into garbage cans, then emptying them into a hog lot and disinfecting the cans. He and a classmate burned used milk cartons and discarded teachers' papers in a burn pile behind the school.

That year when the school pictures came back, Kenneth thought his were good, for a change, and he hoped that "by some small miracle" he'd be able to keep more than just the one 3-by-5-inch picture that he knew would be all his mother could afford.

"The school pictures that were unsold had all been turned back in," he wrote. "I had stalled as long as I could on returning mine … but my little miracle didn't happen."

He'd never thought about what happened to the unsold pictures, until he burned the trash.

"When we poured out one of the cans onto the trash fire, right on top of the heap were my pictures I had returned the day before. I just stood there and watched them slowly curl up from the heat before bursting into flames.

"I could have saved them with no trouble at all and taken them home that afternoon. But for some reason those pictures had lost their shine. I guess I was just too proud, or maybe I thought I would be stealing if I salvaged the school's pictures.

"It's a good thing the smoke was thick and stinging our eyes, because otherwise I would have had to explain to the other free-luncher why I was crying. Later, much later, I realized that my little miracle did happen—but I was just too proud or honest to take advantage of it."

Kenneth Croslin's story is one of some 250 pages of a manuscript that he titled *Calluses and Character: The Life and Times of a Kentucky Sharecropper.* He contacted a few book publishers, but so far all of them have said they are not interested in such stories.

We are, Mr. Croslin, and we thank you for sharing this poignant memory of a long-ago picture day with readers of *Kentucky Living.*

FEBRUARY 2012

Sentimental treasures

Somewhere among the curious artifacts I have accumulated during nearly three-and-a-half decades of wandering around Kentucky, there is a small swatch of fabric from one of actress Vivien Leigh's dresses in the film *Gone with the Wind*.

It would be a great conversation piece—if only I could find it.

Before spring arrives, I may begin a search for many of the missing bits of treasured insignifica I have stashed in drawers, boxes, and who knows where else.

The scraps of Miss Leigh's lavender calico, which she wore as Scarlett O'Hara in many scenes of *Gone with the Wind*, were given to me in 1980 by the late John Friedmann Jr. of Owensboro, who was an assistant to the film's costume designer. Friedmann saved pieces of each star's costume and sent them home to his mother in Daviess County, who made a *Gone with the Wind* quilt.

He insisted that I take a piece of "Scarlett's dress" when I finished an interview with him. I later gave a few scraps to friends and family, and stored the last small swatch someplace for safekeeping. So safe that not even I know its whereabouts.

Somewhere, there is a piece of paling fence that once skirted the log home of the late novelist Janice Holt Giles in rural Adair County. When I visited her home to write of the need to preserve it, the fence was falling down and I picked up part of a broken slat. It may be right at home with a door latch from the corncrib of a long-vanished stock barn on the farm where I was raised.

There is an intricate, tiny chain, carved from a matchstick by a man in Taylor County who left the unstruck match head intact; a copy of a cryptic treasure map famous in eastern Kentucky folkore; a photo of an alleged ghost on the stairs of a Frankfort mansion; and a few frames of 16 mm film shot inside the gold vault at Fort Knox in 1974, when I was among a group of reporters allowed inside the vault to prove that the gold was still there. When the story was edited for a TV newscast, I kept a few frames of the outtakes.

One Easter Sunday long ago, while shooting a TV story about a flood in Bell County, I found in the mud a little girl's new, red Easter slipper with the price tag still attached.

Not wanting to leave it stuck in the mud with the other flood debris, I brought it home and placed it in a box or a drawer where it is still hiding.

Someday when my children sort through my possessions, one of them will likely say, "Why on Earth would Dad keep this?"

One of two reasons, my child: either I could not part with it…or I couldn't find it.

MAY 2012

Myrtle's memories

Myrtle's memories were waiting in my mailbox a few days ago, in a large brown envelope from Calloway County.

Myrtle Rickman Cooper's nephew, Bobby Barron of Murray, had told me they were on the way. Myrtle died in 1996 and Bobby's uncle Jimmy found some of her writings, entitled *Memories*, which Bobby thought I might like to see.

While reading the few pages, I kept wishing that Myrtle's mother, Lucy Rickman, who died in the spring of 1990 at age 96, could have seen the tribute her daughter had written about her soon after her passing.

Myrtle, the fourth of 10 children, three of whom died in infancy, began by describing the Calloway County farmhouse where her family lived when she was born in 1920—three rooms with a porch downstairs, and an unfinished upstairs where some of the children slept under the tin roof. Water was drawn from a cistern that had to have water hauled to it and poured in from a big tank with a rubber hose. No electricity. Myrtle writes:

I recall seeing my mother in the kitchen more than any other place…I have always wondered how she could be everywhere at once, with a baby in her arms and another hanging onto her skirt. She managed to hoe the garden with one baby on a pallet and another in a big box. She would hoe tobacco and cut corn around the edge of the field so that she could keep an eye on the little ones.

I recall many days after I started to school when she would have the washing started before I left and would still be washing when I returned home about three or four o'clock. But, during that time, she had fixed lunch for six or eight men working in the fields, gathered vegetables and prepared them, and picked fruit such as apples, peaches, and blackberries. She never let anything go to waste...

I know my mother could make a gallon of water go further than anybody I know. I think some days now I use more water in one day than we used in months.

Myrtle wrote about homemade toys and good times, church meetings, broomstick skirts her mother made and working in tobacco. Her father, Edd, often borrowed money to buy their school shoes, she said, but always repaid it when his tobacco sold.

We washed on the back porch with two tubs on two chairs turned down. We drew the water, heated it in an iron kettle, scrubbed on a washboard, and hung the clothes on a line and on the garden fence since we never had enough line.

When she finished in the kitchen at night (my mother) always had some patching or sewing to do. I never had a dress made just for me until I was a grown girl...

I never remember hearing my mother complain about not having enough of anything, or having too much work.

AUGUST 2012

Hi-Yo Silver, away!

An old movie handbill from the Lincoln Theater in Stanford, found between the pages of a long-unopened book, takes me back to my cowboy days.

I can still smell the aroma of hot buttered popcorn, gushing from the theater lobby in a rush of cool air, as I plopped down my quarter at the box office beneath the sparkling marquee. In those days, the best I remember, 25 cents would pay for admission to the show, with maybe enough left over for a box of popcorn, a Sugar Daddy, or Sugar Babies.

Color TV was something I had seen only in store windows. And even after we got our first black and white 12-inch RCA, it picked up only one station when conditions were just right. So a trip to the Technicolor picture show was something really special.

Saturday afternoons at the Lincoln always featured a Western, and I would play cowboys relentlessly for weeks after watching Randolph Scott, Lash LaRue, the Lone Ranger on his horse, Silver, or some other hard-riding hero warm up the silver screen with hot lead. You may remember a few of these movies: *Gunsight Ridge*, *The Bushwhackers* or *Guns Don't Argue*.

On Christmas morning at our house, you could hardly see the lights on the tree—much less take a deep breath—in the haze of blue smoke from cap pistols.

Don't let anyone tell you that movies and television do not influence children's behavior.

My father recalled that watching Western movies as a boy in his father's theater at London prompted him to venture westward as a young man with thoughts of becoming a cowboy. Instead, he spent two years prospecting for gold in the mountains of Arizona and herding sheep in New Mexico.

My cowboy days began the moment I learned to say, "Stick 'em up!"

Once, when I was playing cowboys with my younger cousins, Howard and his little sister Donna, they starred in their own version of *The Bushwhackers*. He struck me in the head from behind with the butt of a cap pistol, just as he had seen it done in the movies. Most everything was a blur to me after that, but I imagine the bushwhackers were after my stick horse.

Our mothers just said, "You all stop playing so rough."

Oh, well, I had a whole herd of stick horses where that one came from—Dad's tobacco barn. In fact, there were hundreds, maybe thousands, of tobacco sticks that made perfect stick horses. The good ones were smooth, about 1 inch square and 4 feet long. Generally, I rode a buckskin or palomino, or a pinto if I splashed through enough mud puddles.

I gave up playing cowboys when girls came along, but on my first high school date with Jackie, the girl who is now my wife, we went to the Kentucky Theater to see *Gunfight at the O.K. Corral*.

Maybe it wasn't romantic, but it was the cowboy way.

SEPTEMBER 2013

Room to grow

When I was a kid, most Kentucky schools reopened for classes in September instead of August. And even now a golden, early September morning can evoke memories of those first days back in class.

The smell of freshly oiled pine floors and the toasty warmth of steam radiators in the old school building; mingled aromas of mimeograph ink, the lunchroom, textbooks, chalk dust and, yes, new blue jeans.

Let us linger for a moment with the new jeans.

I suppose we all have our own "school clothes stories." My elementary school wardrobe was mostly hand-me-downs from identical twin cousins who were about five years older than me. But often in late August, I was marched into Sam Robinson's Clothing Store and fitted with denim jeans of about the weight and texture of tent canvas.

The stately, bespectacled Mr. Robinson—wearing a yellow tape measure about his neck—showed no more emotion than if he were dressing a mannequin in the store window.

"I think we'd better go with the larger 'huskies' for him so he'll have plenty of room to grow into them," my mother would insist, and Mr. Robinson would nod in silent agreement.

You'd think he might have been moved by his conscience to say, "Lady, this boy will be lucky to grow into these pants by the time he finishes high school."

Just so you know, I tipped the scales at only 140 pounds my senior year, and if I was still wearing the huskies from fourth grade, you might subtract about 10 pounds from that weight.

In the mirror, my huskies reminded me of two sections of short, fat stovepipe with 4-inch cuffs. As the years passed and I "grew into" the pants, the cuffs could be turned up less.

Some boys wore fancy corduroy pants, which may have scored style points, but had their own problems: namely, noise.

I knew a boy whose sister claims that he once burst through the door after running most of the way home from school in his new corduroys, thinking someone was chasing him—only to discover that it was the sound of his trouser legs rubbing together.

Then there was a high school classmate who often sneaked out behind the school furnace room and had a smoke between classes.

His cigarette lighter was a handful of kitchen matches carried loose in the pockets of his khakis. By the time class was over, he was so desperate for a smoke that he would be on the very edge of his seat, gripping the desktop to get a good jump on the rest of us when the bell rang.

One day, as he lunged forward, his pocket scraped the edge of the desktop and the matches ignited.

His smoke break that morning was spent dancing around the floor in English class as a small cloud of smoke poured from his pants.

He wasn't seriously hurt, but I nearly laughed myself out of my huskies.

JANUARY 2014

Memory lane

The first words of David J. Griffin's story had me hooked: "In a simpler time, kids played outdoors almost every evening."

From then on until I finished his column, whatever else he wrote was a reunion of his memories and my own, chasing each other across the page like children of bygone days playing a game of hide-and-go seek at twilight.

At their best, that is what good nostalgia writers do—sweep us into our own world of remembering, and then lead us gently along forgotten pathways to rediscover pieces of time that are lost in the shadows.

In other columns, Griffin would write about his grandparents' Warm Morning stove, his grandmother's "pocket book," blackberry season, "Pop's" push mower, his first "pizza pie," hubcaps and whitewalls, summer date night circa 1960, "Mommie Katie's" apron, a chicken house, The Little World's Fair at Brodhead, Joyland Park, August football memories, his slingshot, and on and on.

Scanning the story subjects above, your mind may have wandered off to those golden days before lightning bugs, marbles, kick the can and tag were replaced by Xboxes, PlayStations, iPhones and iPads.

We discussed it all a while back when I spent the better part of an afternoon reminiscing with Griffin over a "deluxe" hamburger with fries.

He was born in Rockcastle County and spent a lot of time with his grandparents, Eugene and Katie Stokes, in Mount Vernon. His father, Hobert Griffin, was a taxi driver there, and his mother, Ruby, was a high school English teacher before becoming a full-time mom. David became a chemistry teacher, writing teacher, football and baseball coach. He worked at Campbellsville and Mount Sterling high schools, and then at George Rogers Clark High in Clark County.

He often began chemistry classes with a homespun story related to the subject of his lesson. Many of his former students still thank him for bringing chemistry to life with his stories.

Today, Griffin, 69, and his wife, Kathy, members of Clark Energy Cooperative, live on Furnace Mountain near Stanton in Powell County. His weekly column, *Rockcastle Memories*, in the *Mount Vernon Signal* newspaper, often draws responses from as many as 75 readers a week. More than 50 of his stories are reprinted in his book, *View from the Mountain*.

Griffin reflects that many people today have no concept of having a party line telephone that would ring a certain number of times for each party who shared the line, or of living in a house that was heated with a Warm Morning stove.

"So if you don't write these things down, the majority of young people today will never know about them, because they don't have any reason to talk about them," he says.

The popularity of Griffin's writings reminds all of us that as we grow older, we each have valuable memories to share—of life as we once knew it.

OCTOBER 2014

Voices from the grave

My most poignant memories of years spent tracking stories through eastern Kentucky are images of mourners trudging, single file, up a winding path behind a casket being carried to a small, family cemetery halfway up a mountainside.

Such scenes always brought me to reverence—even in passing—and left me wondering what powerful, unwritten stories lay buried, perhaps lost forever, beneath those gravestones.

Bruce Hopkins of Pike County was determined that many of the stories buried with his kinfolks in the county's Old Prater Cemetery on Greasy Creek would not be forgotten if he could help it.

Through his book, *Spirits in the Field* (Wind Publications), he would bring voices to those whose names are chiseled on weathered markers, and to others in unmarked graves.

As a boy, Hopkins had helped his father clean the grounds and mound up the graves before placing flowers on them every Decoration Day. The many stories he heard back then from old family members meant little to him in his youth, but now, older and in failing health, he felt an almost desperate urge to retrieve those stories—both good and bad—and save them for others.

They were stories of love, violence, hardship and heartbreak; of forefathers who fought for both the Union and Confederacy, some of whom were buried in Old Prater.

He would write of Hooker Hopkins, who, in the 1950s, was often seen wandering in the cemetery with a lantern late at night, searching for the grave of a baby daughter whose burial place he could not find.

He would remember his uncle Avery, who, while dying of Lou Gehrig's disease, struggled to scribble a note to Bruce that said only, "Get gun. Shoot me." Of course, Hopkins could not, and he wonders still if his uncle ever forgave him.

In 1997, Hopkins, a former television reporter and English teacher, was shocked to learn that this cemetery, which his family and others held sacred, lay in the path of a planned rerouting of U.S. Highway 460, and that its graves would have to be relocated.

There were spirits in that lonely field on a high mountainside that called to him "as surely as a dinner bell once called men from the cornfields that had disappeared from Greasy Creek," he says.

His unrelenting, six-year search to recover stories about the 119 he estimated to have been buried there, and his determination to preserve, as best he could, the dignity of their reburial, would eventually lead to his first book, *Spirits in the Field*, then to *Bright Wings to Fly*, *Hearts in Zion* and his current work in progress, *Tell My Father*.

"These books are not about money," insists Hopkins. "They are about preserving stories."

Moreover, his work reminds us all that much of Kentucky's richest history has never been written, but lies buried in countless family cemeteries such as Old Prater, on lonesome mountainsides, or in forgotten, overgrown plots in farm fields.

AUGUST 2018

Our first TV

The old monkey wrench in an antique shop caught my eye and, for a moment, I was 10 years old again—turning the outside TV antenna, a large spider-like contraption that hovered over our central Kentucky farmhouse.

A monkey wrench—for those unfamiliar with the tool—is a heavy, adjustable wrench resembling a large pipe wrench.

Back in the mid-1950s, my dad left a monkey wrench pretty much permanently clamped to the TV antenna pole at our place where, every few days, depending on the wind, someone had to go out and turn the antenna to sharpen the TV reception. This required others to stand at the back door and in front of the TV to relay word when the picture was back to "normal."

The trouble was, often by the time the inside person yelled, "Stop!" whoever was turning the antenna didn't get the word until they had gone too far.

We picked up only one channel on our little 12-inch black-and-white RCA, handed down from an aunt and uncle who had upgraded to a 19- or 21-incher. Those were the days of "rabbit ears," "lead-in wires," "converters" and other terms too technical to be explained here.

Television was just catching on in those days, and my dad—a no-frills guy if there ever was one—had steadfastly insisted he had no use for one. As a boy, he had run the projectors at a movie theater my grandfather operated in London,

Kentucky, and maybe he thought he'd seen enough moving pictures. But the first night we had the TV, he and I watched till sign off near midnight. And early the next morning when I got up, Dad was watching the TV test pattern.

Soon, Chet Huntley and David Brinkley, the entire Mickey Mouse Club, Lawrence Welk's orchestra and Maverick were all part of our family.

What's more, Dad had become an "amateur" TV repairman. Armed only with a screwdriver and an ornate, heirloom hand mirror that my mother kept on the dresser, he would tackle any difficulty that arose with the TV picture. His specialty was fixing problems with the horizontal and vertical hold, which occurred often.

I can see him now in his sock feet, kneeling beside the TV, clutching the mirror in his left hand so as to see the screen while fiddling with controls in the back.

My mother's patience wore thin as frame after snowy frame of Dinah Shore would roll past, then suddenly sideways, until Dad finally got her stabilized.

"That's good!" Mom would say sternly. "Leave it just like that!"

But Dad could never leave well enough alone, so sometimes by the time *Hallmark Hall of Fame* came on, we already had our own drama underway around the dysfunctional little 12-inch screen.

I'm telling you—if today's fancy flat-screens are all you've ever watched, you don't know much about television.

Call me crazy, but I still have Dad's screwdriver and Mom's hand mirror just in case there's trouble.

JANUARY 2019

The stories Sarah saved

We often hear someone say, "I wish I'd written them down," when trying to remember stories told by a departed friend or family member.

Sarah Humes, 87, of rural Shelby County actually did write them down when her late husband, Ernest, who died in 2003, recalled incidents from his boyhood during the Great Depression years.

One of six children of a sharecropper family in Spencer County, he remembered times when food was scarce, and Christmases when there was not even a piece of candy. Yet, among sad memories there were some smiles—which brings us to a trade that Ernest made with another little boy on the playground at Finchville school.

"I was having a good time on the swing, and there was another boy watching me—and kept wanting my swing—but I was not about to give it up. After swinging for a while, I told him I would sell it to him for a dime. And he said, OK, he would pay me.

"After school I went home with this boy to get my money. After playing for quite a while he finally agreed to go ask his mother for a dime. In a little while, she brought the dime to me and said, 'Now, don't you sell him that swing anymore.'

"This was the very first money that I ever remember having, and it felt so good, because I felt this was a lot of money, and I guess it really was a lot for that year, 1929."

Ernest's words paint a stark picture of why, in many photographs of schoolchildren during those desperate years, almost no one is smiling.

"When the weather began to get cool, I didn't have any shoes to wear. One day the weather was real cool, and I wore an overcoat to school, but no shoes. It looked funny to the other children, and some of them made fun of me. The next day I left the coat at home, and I guess I didn't look so bad. No one said anything."

Often left alone, Ernest, his three brothers and two sisters learned to take care of themselves.

"When our parents were gone, we really turned on. I remember pouring water on the kitchen linoleum so we could slide on it. We would start running and hit that water and slide across that kitchen and just have the best time. When we saw our parents coming, we started mopping water and getting everything in place."

Most of their meat consisted of wild game, but Ernest remembered once when his dad "borrowed" a neighbor's lamb.

"Of course, our neighbor never knew we had taken this animal. I think my dad was an honest man, but when you need food for your family, you do what is necessary to feed them. This is the only time I ever knew of where my dad took something that belonged to someone else. You cannot imagine how hard things were in the 1930s."

AUGUST 2020

Car talk

A song on the radio took me back for a moment to high school days, behind the wheel of my favorite car—a 1957 Chevy Bel Air.

There's A Moon Out Tonight by an early doo-wop group called The Capris, was a bittersweet flashback. Often, in the middle of one of those great songs, the '57's radio would suddenly go silent, and I'd have to give the dashboard a good thumping with my fist, near the speaker, to restart the music, usually just in time to hear the ending.

It played havoc with the mood on a date.

No, the '57 wasn't perfect, but in her prime she was a looker. And ever since she parallel parked with me during my driver's test, she's owned a little piece of my heart. I loved her ivory hardtop, her metallic copper body (which some Chevy paint guru named "Sierra Gold,") her charming tailfins, the big gold "V" on the front and back, and her 283-cubic-inch V-8 with a four-barrel carburetor that was forever whispering, "make me go faster!"

In reflection, maybe that wasn't a good idea, considering that my high school sweetheart, Jackie, who is now my wife, has no recollection of seat belts in the '57. She does have all-too-vivid recall of trouble with a door latch, which I tried to remedy with a "do-it-myself" shortcut to avoid unnecessary expense.

The passenger door would not stay closed, and that can be tricky on hard left turns. So I came up with a twofold safety idea of tying the ends of a sturdy nylon rope to each arm rest. I called it, "the rope stretched across the front seat." You know it today as "passive restraint."

Jackie was fond of the '57, but fussed about the yellow rope, and seemed uncomfortable with tying herself in when I picked her up, then simply untying the two half-hitches when we got to a movie.

She complained until I eventually had the door latch repaired, but I don't think the speaker was ever fixed. Otherwise, I would not still resist a mild urge to clench my fist when cruising down memory lane and a favorite oldie comes on the radio.

Of course, there are other unforgettable vehicles besides the '57 in time's rearview mirror, most notably an old Jeep that I still miss from my days on the farm. But that's another story. And I'm guessing that, by now, you're lost in your own car and truck memories—which I welcome for a future back page.

A dear-departed friend used to tell me about the car he drove on his first date with the pretty girl who later became his wife.

When he opened the passenger door to let her in, the door fell off!

I wish I had been there to help. I still carry a crescent wrench, a roll of duct tape and a strong piece of nylon rope for such emergencies.

APRIL 2021

Before smartphones

When Elsie Newman Carpenter became a telephone operator in the rural Logan County community of Auburn in 1948, a phone call from Auburn to the county seat of Russellville, 10 miles away, was long distance.

Most callers were still using wall-mounted crank telephones that were encased in oak boxes about 2 feet tall and 9 inches wide.

Elsie, who was then 15, was paid 35 cents an hour after school to handle calls through the central switchboard for Southern Continental Telephone Company. She wore a headset and sat at a vertical panel of 150 phone jacks, taking calls and connecting them with their party by inserting a plug on a cord into a jack. Many knew her from her weekend job at the local Houchen's Market and would call her by name.

"They'd just ring and say, 'Get me so-and-so on the line,' you know. Back then people didn't call just to talk like we do nowadays. You had to have something important enough to call—or you didn't use the phone," Elsie says.

Phone numbers were simpler then, from one to three digits. Elsie, at age 89, still remembers a few customers' numbers.

The manager of the telephone exchange and his family lived in the back of the building where the switchboard was situated. Their son, who was about 12, and two of his friends sometimes played ball in the same room where Elsie was working.

"Oh my goodness! You talk about a mess, trying to hear what's going on with the switchboard, and trying to keep them quiet."

In those days, often as many as seven or eight customers might share the same line, known as a "party line," which sometimes led to colorful stories about customers who listened in, or "eavesdropped," on other callers.

If someone called to report a fire, Elsie could activate the town's emergency siren from the switchboard.

"Then the volunteer firemen would call me to see where the fire was."

If Auburn's two doctors had dinner plans or other engagements that took them away from home after office hours, they left word with Elsie where they could be reached.

Elsie worked as an operator until 1951, shortly before she married and began life as a housewife and mother of a son and daughter. A lifelong consumer-member of Pennyrile Electric, she's now in her 46th year of coordinating Red Cross blood drives with local Church Women United, and has been recognized with numerous honors, including Citizen of the Year.

Not long ago, during a trip to Bowling Green with her son, she heard him ask his smartphone for the phone number of a local pharmacy, and a female voice instantly responded with the information. Elsie smiled, perhaps pondering how phones have progressed since her days long ago on the switchboard.

Yes, Elsie, your son's nifty smartphone can answer many questions—but can it tell him where his doctor is having dinner tonight?

MAY 2021

Iconic barn advertising

While I was traveling down U.S. Highway 31E in Hart County a few months back, the sight of a weathered old barn, partially hidden behind a grove of trees just below the LaRue County line, called back a memory and a smile.

Still visible on the side of the barn facing the highway were dim letters in white and yellow against what once was a black background, "CHEW MAIL POUCH TOBACCO—Treat Yourself To The Best."

The master of these fading brushstrokes of barn advertising, Harley Warrick of Belmont, Ohio, passed away in November 2000 after a 55-year career in which he and his helpers painted or retouched more than 20,000 Mail Pouch barns in 13 states, including Kentucky. He initialed and dated some of his work. And yes, he chewed Mail Pouch.

When I spoke with him by phone a year and a half before he died, he guessed that most of the Mail Pouch barns in Kentucky must have been "in pretty bad shape" by then since he hadn't been back to repaint them much after the 1965 Highway Beautification Act eliminated many roadside billboards. The act was later amended to exempt Mail Pouch and a few other folk heritage barns.

During the peak of barn advertising, from the early to mid-20th century, barn art across Kentucky and many other states urged passing motorists on busy roads to try various products, or to "See Rock City," or visit Lookout Mountain, Cudjo's Cave and others.

Mail Pouch barns were once more numerous in some eastern Kentucky counties where chewing tobacco was popular among coal miners who could not smoke in deep mines.

By the time Harley Warrick was laid to rest, his Mail Pouch barns had already taken their place as rural American cultural icons, favorite subjects of artists and photographers.

One of those photographers, Bill Eichelberger of Fort Thomas in Campbell County, has been photographing Mail Pouch barns since the mid-1980s. While a history major at Northern Kentucky University, he developed an interest in preserving images of cultural landmarks.

His earliest Mail Pouch barn searches in Kentucky took him into Mason and Fleming counties, then down U.S. Highway 27 into Pendleton and Harrison counties. He eventually canvassed much of Indiana and Ohio, and central and eastern Kentucky. Many of his 240 or so Mail Pouch barn photos, along with those of other photographers, may be seen on the websites, mailpouchbarnstormers.org and LandmarkHunter.com.

He guesses there could be as many as 40 to 45 Mail Pouch barns remaining in Kentucky, but says most are in disrepair, their paint fading, their roofs and boards ravaged by weather and age.

Yet, thanks to Eichelberger and others, today's vanishing remnants of Harley Warrick's memorable roadside art will survive in pictures for many more generations. As Warrick said when we last talked, the barns are getting more popular now that they're disappearing.

FEBRUARY 2022

A toy story

How much can you carry in an antique, 3-inch-long metal pickup truck with no wheels?

A ton of memories.

Louis Singleton, 91, first told me the story of his toy truck 20 years ago, and last fall I asked him to tell me again.

He cradled the little truck in his hand as we traveled back to the early 1940s when the country was still recovering from the Great Depression and had just been drawn into World War II. Times were tough for many families.

Louis's father worked as a section hand for the Louisville & Nashville Railroad, and Louis, his sister, two brothers and their parents lived near the L&N tracks in western Shelby County in a home that was made from two converted train cars.

Life may have been hard for some, but for Louis and his siblings it seemed a wonderful adventure.

Nearly every day they walked up the railroad tracks to a small dump site off the beaten path where they searched through the trash for toys that had been discarded by city folks.

"About all the toys we had were what we found in that dump," he says.

Stray marbles, injured dolls and other toy misfits fell into loving hands among the children. Louis's 10-year-old brother, Kenneth, found a perfectly good red wagon, and Louis found the small metal truck with no wheels. It was red at the time, but he later painted it green. It wore scars of a rough life, but the notch cut in the cab didn't matter to Louis when he was guiding it along make-believe roads in the dirt where the children played.

As they walked to the dump one day, Kenneth was pulling his red wagon and the rear wheels got caught on a rail as they crossed the tracks. While working to free it, they heard a train approaching, and all got off the track except Kenneth, who stayed, determined to save the wagon.

"That old engineer was hanging way out the window hollering, 'Get off the track little boy!' Turn the wagon loose!'"

Kenneth ran to safety only seconds before his wagon was crushed by the locomotive. He was heartbroken—until the engineer stopped the train the next day and stepped off the engine with a brand new Radio Flyer wagon to replace the one that had been lost.

In those days the freight train crew cooked on a coal-burning stove in the caboose and often stopped to share their food with Louis's family. The family, likewise, shared their meals with a kindly old bearded man, known as "Rail-walking John," who traipsed along the tracks, balancing himself on a rail with a walking stick.

Many of the people and treasured moments of those bygone days are now resting in the shadows of time. But a ton of memories come tumbling from the tiny green truck with no wheels when Louis Singleton lifts it from the little box where he's kept it all these years.

JUNE 2022

Sweet footnotes

The small metal box had been stored away among some of my mother's possessions since soon after her passing several years ago.

It's a 4-by-6-inch index card file like those many of our teachers kept on their desks during the pre-digital age. Inside, I found a collection of my mom, Lucille Crawford's, dessert recipes going back to when I was a kid. Most were in her handwriting on random scraps of paper.

Apple Orchard Delight was written on the back of a letter from my Uncle Harry, who lived near Bush in Laurel County. It was dated February 17, 1960.

"Well, did you have a big snow?" he began. "We had one that averaged around 12 inches. Some drifts were three feet deep I guess." Many people there had the flu, he said, but he and Aunt Cinda had been well so far. They needed to get out to the grocery for a few things.

Family and friends were well-represented in the recipe box. Effie's Pie, from my aunt Effie, began with 2 cups brown sugar, 1/2 cup butter and 3 egg yolks—so you know it had to be good. Bessie's Buttermilk Pie was from one of mom's dear friends.

A recipe saved on a bank memo from Danville was for Impossible Pie on one side and Transparent Pie on the other. I never remember seeing either pie.

My dad, a longtime consumer-member of Inter-County Energy, had done some figuring on the back of mom's Banana Fritters recipe, but there was no clue what all the numbers meant.

Somewhere in thumbing through recipes for the likes of Luscious Squares, Cherry Delights, Jelly Pie, 10-Eggwhite Cake and many others, I realized that—beyond the origins of my triglyceride reserves—I was glimpsing sweet footnotes of family history.

A page torn from a small desktop calendar dated Saturday, August 3, 1968, and used for a Hush Puppies recipe, would have been one day after my parents' first grandchild, our oldest son, was born.

The Pulled Cream Candy recipe stirred memories of the old marble-top wash stand where mom always poured hot cream taffy to cool before pulling. Her instructions at the end said: *"Pour on marble til it is cool enough to pull. Pull until it starts leaving your hands."*

Pullers would thoroughly clean and butter their hands before pulling ropes of the warm taffy. Dad once began pulling before the taffy was sufficiently cooled, and put on a memorable show trying to juggle hot taffy and pull at the same time.

I was probably barely out of coloring books when mom saved a clipping from the November 1953 issue of *Rural Kentuckian* magazine containing a recipe for White Fruit Cake from Mrs. John Taul of Route 3, Hardinsburg. White fruit cake would become one of my favorites, and years later the *Rural Kentuckian* would become *Kentucky Living*—whose back page seemed a likable place for this little reflection.

Thanks for the memories, Mom.

NOVEMBER 2022

For whom the dinner bells toll

Surely somewhere among the distant echoes in the great beyond, a dinner bell still rings.

Time was, in decades past, when many Kentucky farmyards had a dinner bell on a post near the house—used mostly to call workers from the fields at noon. Much farm work was still done quietly with horses and mules in those days, when a bell could still be heard. Old farmers have told how some mules would stop working and immediately head for the house when the dinner bell rang.

Before phone service reached many rural areas, neighbors in most communities knew the continued ringing of a dinner bell, at any hour other than noon or suppertime, usually meant someone needed help.

The late Clorine Lawson of Barren County once told me her family frantically rang the dinner bell in 1910 when her aunt was choking on one of those picture buttons that were often used in political campaigns of that day. Neighbors came running to help, and her aunt coughed up the button before the doctor arrived.

Author and historian Todd Moberly of Madison County, a consumer-member of Blue Grass Energy, recalls his sixth-grade teacher telling about her grandmother's small dog that was trained to pull the rope and ring a dinner bell that was anchored to a tree. When the grandmother fell and broke her hip, the little dog rang the bell and alerted the neighbors.

I remember a visit with reclusive Trimble County artist and writer Harlan Hubbard, when we met at Plowpoint Landing on the Indiana shore of the Ohio River. Across the river, at Payne Hollow, Harlan and his wife, Anna, led a solitary, back-to-nature existence in a remote homestead overlooking the Kentucky shoreline. There was a dinner bell to ring on the Indiana shore, and Harlan rowed his johnboat across the river to meet me.

James Riley of Marshall County, a consumer-member of West Kentucky RECC, says when he was a boy in the rural settlement of Sharpe, a neighbor who lived alone attached a lightweight rope about 50 feet long to her dinner bell, and ran it through a window to sound the alarm if she needed help.

The late Mary Lee of McCreary County said years ago that, as children, she and her siblings were told to ring the dinner bell to alert her father, a beekeeper, when the bees were swarming.

Television journalist Charles Kuralt, who hitchhiked through Kentucky as a teenager and later returned numerous times to film his popular *On The Road* segments for the *CBS Evening News*, included in an audio collection a memory of the old bell on a post in the yard of his maternal grandparents' farmhouse in rural North Carolina. The grandfather continued a tradition begun by his father of ringing the bell every Christmas Eve to invite anyone nearby to have dinner with the family.

I'm thinking we could use a few more dinner bells these days.

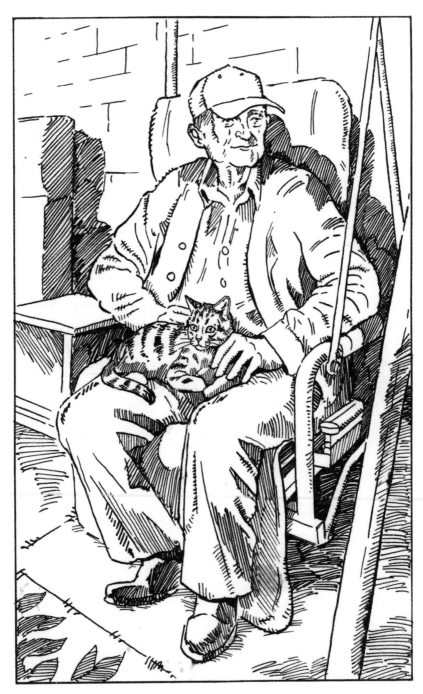

One-of-a kind dog, page 42

II

Love

JANUARY 2012

One-of-a-kind dog

Had my father Delbert Crawford lived until the 20th of this month he'd have been 103 years old. We lost him to pneumonia last April.

Thinking of him just now, I am remembering how he continued to savor life during his last months, even as age stole most of his eyesight, his hearing, and his mind.

When he no longer could see to work crossword puzzles or giant word jumbles, he shifted his interest to moon phases and what time the moon came up each night, waiting at certain windows to watch. "Did you see how pretty the moon was tonight?" he'd ask on the phone. He even made a study of what time each evening the mercury vapor streetlights came on.

His last summer with us—as his senses dimmed to a flicker—he often spent hours sitting in the swing on the patio, but rarely had much to say.

Then one afternoon, out of nowhere, a disheveled tomcat wandered straight up to the swing, jumped into Dad's lap, began purring, and curled up to be petted.

My mother, Lucille, was amazed at the transformation that suddenly came over Dad. He began laughing and talking again, to the big gray cat with white feet.

No one around the neighborhood had ever seen the cat, which had been declawed and neutered, and its owner could not be found.

My mother called it a miracle. Dad called it a dog.

We never knew if he really thought the cat was a dog, or if, because he'd always loved dogs so much, he just imagined it was. We named it Dog.

One day Dad asked, "Have you ever seen a dog like this?" I said, "No, Dad, I really think you've got one-of-a-kind here."

Some days my mother would hear him talking to Dog in the swing, telling him what a pretty and good dog he was, and singing to him that old hymn, *In the Sweet By and By.*

My folks had never allowed animals in the house, except for a baby lamb born one night back on the farm when the temperature was zero. But when winter came and Dad could no longer sit in the swing with Dog, Mom relented and allowed Dog into the house for long visits.

When Dad went to the hospital last spring and never came home, Dog began to lose weight and seemed lost for a few months.

At Dad's funeral there was a picture of him and Dog in the swing, and John Kolasa sang *In the Sweet By and By* a cappella.

Dog has remained a special friend to my mother, who continues to care for him, and spends time each day loving him and playing with him as my dad did. She always tells him how happy we are that he found us, how very much my dad loved him, and what a one-of-a-kind dog he will always be to our family.

APRIL 2012

Curtain call

Overhearing a discussion of prom dress prices the other day brought to mind a story I had heard from Alene Horner many years ago.

Alene, 85, a retired teacher who now lives in southern Indiana, spent her early childhood in a small, now-vanished Whitley County coal camp called Bon Jellico. Her paternal grandparents, Richard and Vina Kirklin, lived close by.

From the time she was a toddler, Alene treasured the moments spent with her grandmother, an even-tempered, sturdy little woman who wore her hair done up in a bun.

Alene often sat on Grandma's lap and helped her milk Star, the family cow. On some visits her grandmother would give Alene a needle, thread and thimble and let her help stitch quilts. The stitches may have been removed later, Alene supposes, but helping to create something so pretty instilled in her an early love of sewing.

Her mother died when Alene was 14, and around that time the mine closed and her grandparents moved to Savoy, not far from Williamsburg. Alene stayed with them on weekends and during the summers until she finished high school, then she came to live with them and entered Cumberland College, now University of the Cumberlands, in Williamsburg.

She walked to and from classes each day from their little white house in the country. It was nothing fancy, but it was always well-kept and cozy, with starched, lace curtains hung from the windows in two of the rooms, and love in every corner.

Alene was sweeping the front porch one morning just before Christmas when her grandfather came walking from town with a large bag under his arm and a twinkle in his eyes.

Not until after he died three years later would Alene learn that—without prompting from her grandmother—the old miner had picked out the large cloth doll left under the tree for her that Christmas morning. It is still among her most treasured keepsakes.

She had never heard of a prom dress in those days, but occasionally there were costume parties and other dress-up events at school. When she was 17, she wanted to go to a college costume party, but she had no dress and there was no money to buy one, so she gave up on the idea.

Then one afternoon she came home from school to find that her grandmother had cut up her prized lace curtains from the dining room window, along with one of her best cotton slips, and had made a pretty dress, an apron, and bonnet for Alene to wear, dressed as Little Bo Peep, on that one special night.

"I'm sure that I cried," Alene recalls. "I still get real teary when I think about it."

In this cluttered world of store-bought memories that often fade so soon, there is something of lasting value in the story of Alene Kirklin Horner's most unforgettable dress—made so long ago with lace curtains and a grandmother's love.

FEBRUARY 2013

Straight from the heart

Valentine's Day rarely passes that I don't think of my old friend Sam Denny's last valentine to his wife, Pat.

It wasn't really a formal valentine, but it was a message straight from his heart.

Waller Sam Denny grew up in Lancaster and met Pat Weinedel of Louisville when they were students at Centre College in Danville during the late 1940s.

She was a freshman and he was a sophomore four years older who had already served a tour in the Navy. They married in 1949.

He had green eyes, blond curly hair, and was very athletic; not tall, maybe 5-foot-8, Pat said. "He was a barrel of fun, and there wasn't a dishonest bone in his body." They had two sons, Jim and Sam, with whose permission I share this story.

After their father died in 1997 following a long, debilitating illness, Pat found among his personal papers a note written years earlier: "To be opened in the event of my death."

"Memo to Patricia W. Denny–

"Pat, if you ever have occasion to read this perhaps you will think that I want to think for you even after I am gone. There are many things I would like to say as I sit at the office typing this memo. Some of the things I wish to cover are things I have

thought about for a long time and have never gotten around to putting in writing.

"I do not say this to make you sad, but to make you feel better. I have always loved you. With my perfectionist-type personality and short temper I feel that I have never been capable of giving you the love to which you were entitled. Again, I say I have loved you and am proud of you as a wife and as a mother.

"…Once I am gone I want my memory to hold no strings on you. I would of course want you to remember me as a happy part of your past, but not as a sad part of your future. What I am trying to say is this, lead a normal life—if a guy worthy of you comes along—marry him. If you get an opportunity to enjoy life in some way don't be bound by tradition. Remember this, the past was fun and a wonderful part of your life, but it is the past…Even if we had no children I would feel the way I have stated above, but with children it is all the more important. They should remember you as you are capable of being—enjoy them and enjoy life.

Love, W.S."

Pat said she loved him that much more after reading his note. She never remarried, but did share a close friendship with a widower at her church who had been a dear friend of Sam's. It was a friendship made sweeter because of Sam's last valentine.

Pat Denny died in January 2012 at the age of 82.

MAY 2013

Dirt is good for the soul

The coming of Mother's Day stirs dusty memories of those long-lost—pre-video game—years when many children, including me, spent most of our waking hours playing in dirt. Our mothers should have earned the lifetime Good Housekeeping Award for cleaning us up before bedtime.

Maybe you remember.

Dirt wasn't welcome in our house, but I never recall Mom punishing me for getting dirty. Talking back to her, on the other hand, always landed me in the fearsome shadow of a little maple tree in the backyard whose switches brought tears to my eyes even before they touched me.

My early years were largely grounded in dirt. A neighbor girl once talked me into sampling a slice of her mud pie, so I guess you could say dirt was in my blood.

Dad was a farmer, and when I was still too young to help set tobacco, I often sat at the end of the field, playing in the dirt. When he plowed corn ground, I followed behind in the furrow, picking up fishing worms.

If the folks who now live at our old place knew where to dig, they might start a nice marble collection with the swirls, cat eyes, and bumblebees I left buried there. In our pastures I got to know doodlebugs, click beetles, and the loveable tumblebug from the ground up.

Digging in the front yard one day I struck pay dirt—a tomahawk-like American Indian relic of dark, smooth stone that Dad called a "skinning rock."

Then there was the winter day when I had been sick for a while and was sitting with my toy tractor, plow and disk harrow, looking out the window and wishing I could play in the dirt.

Mom passed by and must have known what I was thinking. To my surprise, she appeared in the doorway with a gallon bucket of the finest dirt you ever saw, and poured it out for me to play in—right there on the old linoleum floor that looked like a braided rug. Then she gave me an understanding smile and left the room.

My mother, Lucille Crawford, has done many kind things for me over the years, but few have stuck in my mind so clearly, or so dearly.

Years later, when I asked what had caused her sudden change of heart that day, she answered simply, "You can't plow without dirt."

This spring, a time when Mom would ordinarily be outdoors working in her flower garden, she is mostly indoors, weakened by chemotherapy treatments. Now, I am the one who passes the doorway and sees her gazing wistfully out the window.

I have never tied a ribbon around an old gallon bucket filled with potting soil, but this Mother's Day I may try. I might attach a few packets of flower seeds and a note that reads:

"You can't raise flowers without dirt. Maybe you remember. I sure do."

Love you Mom.

NOVEMBER 2013

Social networking 1925

Long before romance was kindled through texting and tweeting, Virginia V. Kilfoy, who worked at a pants factory near her home in Mountain Grove, Missouri, used a more personal approach to find the love of her life, Spencer County, Kentucky, farm boy Raymond Thomas.

The year was 1925. Both Virginia and Raymond were in their mid-20s and still single. WSM Radio in Nashville would debut a new show that year called *The Grand Ole Opry*. If singers on the *Opry* had known Raymond and Virginia's story, they might have composed a great country song about the couple's courtship.

It all began the day Virginia and several other women at the pants factory were discussing who might wear the riding pants they were making, and they came up with a novel idea: each would write her name and address on a small slip of paper and tuck it inside the pocket of the pants they made, hoping, Virginia said, to catch a lonely cowboy or two.

Back in Spencer County, the pants with Virginia's name in the pocket were purchased by Raymond's brother, Everett. He was already married, but he passed the name on to Raymond, who wrote to Virginia. Then she wrote back, and he wrote back, and they continued writing for two years.

Raymond boasted in one letter that his potato crop was so big that he could feed four people with one potato. When Virginia showed the letter to other women at work, they began calling him "the big potato man from the South."

At Christmas in 1927, Raymond boarded a train to Missouri for his first face-to-face visit with Virginia. He later claimed that after she saw him, she begged him to take her back to Kentucky. But Virginia said that was a lot of baloney.

She said that nearly a year later, a few weeks before Christmas 1928, he began signing his letters "Love Raymond," and when he returned to Missouri that Christmas they were married on December 27.

Although they started with only a few hundred dollars, they worked hard and were soon able to buy a 70-acre farm between Taylorsville and Elk Creek that was to be their home for life.

The slip of paper on which Virginia had written her name and address would vanish with time, but the marriage lasted until she and Raymond were parted by death. She died in the summer of 1986 at 86. He died in early 1992 at 91.

Their grandson, Eddie, now farms the old homeplace, and their son, Robert, and his wife, Helen, live next door.

The sweet William that Virginia planted in the front yard and nurtured all those years is now gone, but two of the maple trees that she and Raymond planted—and in whose shade they spent their last summers together—are still there in the yard, monuments to a young Missouri woman's long-ago search for a lonesome cowboy.

FEBRUARY 2017

An unforgettable love story

The last note she got from him before he left for the war was a large Valentine card on which he had written, "I love you, I love you, xoxoxo."

It was 1951, and Steve Palas, a young soldier from Lumberton, North Carolina, in tank training at Fort Knox, was soon to leave for Korea. He had met Pat Osborne at the USO club in Louisville where she was a volunteer, sharing dances with young soldiers.

She was about the prettiest girl he'd ever seen—and the best dancer. He wasn't much of a dancer, but he felt like Fred Astaire when she was in his arms. If theirs wasn't love at first sight, it was close. And before he shipped out, when he asked if she'd marry him when he got home from Korea, Pat said "yes."

Her mother bitterly opposed her plans to marry a soldier who was going off to war, but Pat promised Steve she would wait.

No letters came for many months. Pat heard that he had been assigned to the battle zone, where he was a tank commander with the Third Armored Divison, and she feared the worst.

She tried to go on with everyday life, but sometimes during work hours at a bank she'd go into a room alone and cry.

Much later, she learned her mother had intercepted three letters from Steve that were written before his capture by the North Koreans. Receiving no answers to his letters, Steve assumed that maybe Pat had found someone else. He spent seven months as a POW and had lost 70 pounds by the time he was freed and returned to the States.

Pat was on a trip to Tennessee with her mother at the time, but Steve called her father and learned that Pat had been waiting.

The two were married about one year later, in June of 1954, and settled in Louisville, where both later worked in the insurance business and where Steve was also a high school football referee. They had three children.

Steve, now age 88, remembers that she held on to the Valentine from 1951 for many years, and he wishes he could find it now.

On their 50th wedding anniversary, their daughter, Vickie, with the assistance of an antique car owner, arranged to have Steve and Pat chauffeured to their anniversary party in a 1953 white-over-baby blue Chevy Bel Air just like their first car. He played a cassette tape of Nat King Cole singing "their"song—*Unforgettable.*

By the time their 60th anniversary came along, Pat was suffering from dementia. Steve cared for her at home as long as possible before she was hospitalized.

The girl who had waited for him all those months, with only a Valentine, died with her head on his shoulder in September 2015.

"She was my rock," he said. "There's never been anyone else in my life that lit it up the way she did."

FEBRUARY 2018

Love letters

"**D**earest little girl," his letters began.

Owen Thomas Yates, a lovesick World War I soldier from Kentucky, was writing to his sweetheart, Eunice Centers, who had stolen his heart back in Allen County.

"Tom" had grown up on a farm in Barren County; Eunice on a farm just across the line in Allen County. They met while walking home from church not long before he was drafted in 1917.

"I don't know much about other red-headed girls, but I do know that there is one red-headed girl who is the best little girl in the world and the only girl in the world for me," he wrote in one of his many letters to her over the next two years.

Eunice saved all the letters, which eventually were passed on to the Yates children and later copied by a cousin. The originals are now keepsakes of the Yates's grandson, Greg Dunn, an attorney in Cave City, who shared them with me.

"You seem dearer to me every day I am away from you ... I wouldn't give one smile from you for every woman in France," Tom wrote from Le Mans on a February day 100 years ago.

Although Eunice answered faithfully, her letters often did not reach him for months.

Only one of the letters she wrote—returned to her "undeliverable"—still exists. It reads, in part: "Tom, I dreamed the other night that you had come home, and were here (but woke to find it only a dream), may the time speedily come when my dream shall come true…I am as ever your little girl. By-By-Dearest."

Despite their love for each other, both struggled with doubt from time to time.

"Eunice, I could not blame you if you found someone you could love better than you do me, who is not in the army and can be with you, but life would be very unhappy for me if it wasn't for the thoughts of a little blue-eyed girl down in Allen County that I love, and trust someday will be my wife…"

World War I ended in late 1918, but Tom was not discharged from the Army until September 1919, two years after he was drafted. Then he was met with heartbreaking news. He had tuberculosis, and doctors said that his best hope was to move to a drier climate. He spent two years living alone in New Mexico before he was well, but never stopped writing to Eunice, pledging his love.

"Eunice, I am coming after you," he wrote in November 1921. "I have waited a long time … "

They were married on December 31, 1921, and lived in Albuquerque, New Mexico, for eight more years. They had three children before moving back to Allen County, where they led a happy life together on a 220-acre farm on the Barren River.

Tom died in 1969; Eunice in 1990, but their love still speaks to us in letters saved by the "dearest little girl."

SEPTEMBER 2018

Letters to Charlie

The last thing Mike remembers was walking out the door of his home in 2014 on his way to a hospital—suddenly unable to see in his right eye.

About one year later, he regained consciousness in a nursing home, not knowing who he was, where he was or what happened. A stroke had taken him to death's gate and had stolen his memory,

Much of his memory returned in time, but he still has difficulty reading, and often struggles to find the right words in conversation. The right words are especially important to him now as he writes "letters to Charlie," his 2-year-old grandson, who was born about the time Mike left the nursing home and returned to his 60-acre Franklin County farm.

Aware that he now is at increased risk of another stroke from which he might not recover, Mike is passing along some of his life lessons to Charlie, his only grandchild, in a collection of handwritten letters.

There is grandfatherly advice on daily living, observations on human behavior, gardening tips, family stories and many heartfelt expressions of affection:

"Hello Charlie! I am your paternal grandfather ... born May 19, 1949. I am thrilled to be your grandfather and am so excited to have you!

"The purpose of these letters is to not only inform you about your family history, but to give you insight into the many opportunities that you will have throughout your

life … also to avoid the many mistakes in judgment that a young man can make that can cause negative effects in your life, as I want you to learn from my errors and those things I have done correctly …

"I may not live long enough to spend a lifetime with you, and I want you to know me through these letters."

In nearly 50 pages so far, Mike, a retired director of Occupational Safety and Health for Kentucky, explains to Charlie how difficult life was for his ancestors, the importance of studying the Bible, going to church and getting a good education and the dangers of drugs and alcohol. He tells of a distant uncle who, in the late 1800s, owned a farm that is now part of the Kentucky Horse Park, and he offers thoughts on healing a heartache.

"One of the hardest things to face in our lives is a broken heart, and through our lives we will face several … The pain always becomes settled. At first it is all we think about, but as time goes on it will get better.

"Surround yourself with friends. It helps. Work helps too but try not to just think about it."

Mike expects it will be years before Charlie reads the letters in a bound journal, but they'll be waiting.

"The farm is being set up so that you get to take it over either after college or when in your early 20s …

"I love you, and we will be together in another life!

"Pappaw."

NOVEMBER 2021

Love in a bottle

Henry Rowlett liked fishing the Ohio River near Wise's Landing in Trimble County where his family farmed.

One autumn day in 1920 he noticed, floating in the river, a bottle with a message inside. The exact wording has been lost in time, but it's known to have listed the name and address of Cynthia Barnes of Cynthiana, Kentucky.

Henry wrote to Cynthia that he'd found her message, perhaps along with information about himself and how he came to discover the bottle—which she said she had tossed into the river during a visit to Maysville more than 100 miles upstream. The two exchanged letters for several months until Henry's girlfriend, Gracie, put a stop to his writing. But the message in the bottle had only begun its romantic journey.

Henry's brother, Creed, a farmer who lived nearby, had lost his wife, Bertha, the mother of their four children, from injuries she suffered when thrown from a horse. Their youngest, Howard, who was almost 2, had been sent to live with his grandparents on a nearby farm, but Creed, with the help of other family, was doing the best he could to care for Roy, 9, Laura, 11, and Lena, 12.

By now you may have guessed that Henry passed along Cynthia's address to his widowed brother who began exchanging letters with the young woman in Cynthiana.

Sharon Rowlett of Campbellsburg, a granddaughter of Creed Rowlett and consumer-member of Shelby Energy, says Creed and Cynthia exchanged letters for a few months before deciding to meet in Louisville.

Cynthia had never been married, and neither she nor Creed had seen a picture of the other, but felt they knew each other well through their letters.

In April 1921, Creed boarded a steamboat at Wise's Landing as Cynthia made her way from Cynthiana to a hotel in Louisville where they'd arranged to meet in the lobby. Cynthia had written that she'd be wearing a black hat and coat; he wrote that he'd be wearing his "winter hat," the only one he had, he later explained.

They found each other that day, and married in Louisville before returning to Trimble County by steamboat.

Back at home in the large farmhouse, as the story was often told by his children, Creed sat all four of them on the bed as he and Cynthia took their seats in two straight-back chairs, facing them. Then he told them that Cynthia was their new mother, and that they were to call her "Mom" and show her respect. As far as is known, Sharon Rowlett says, they all enjoyed a pleasant, happy life as a family, and later added another daughter, LaVelle.

The marriage lasted 56 years. Creed passed away in the fall of 1971, and Cynthia several years later. Their many grandchildren are left to tell the story of how, a century ago, one of their ancestors found love in a bottle floating in the Ohio River.

FEBRUARY 2023

Words of love

For what it's worth—and with great respect for the gifted poets and lyricists who've tried to define love through the ages—the simple, genuine thoughts on the subject from children and the elderly have left the most memorable impressions with me.

Among their words are several I've saved from a long-ago class of fifth-graders at Wright Elementary School in Shelby County, who shared their thoughts on love one Valentine's Day.

"Love is when your grandfather kisses you goodbye for the last time," wrote Ashley.

Strider wrote, "Love is when your mom stays home from work when you are sick."

And Erin said, "Love is when I hold my cat and she falls asleep in my arms."

Jackie Daffron, who once had a home for orphaned and injured Raggedy Ann and Andy dolls in Monticello, sent a valentine with children's definitions of love. A little boy named Billy said, "When someone loves you, the way they say your name is different."

Years ago, workers at a Hodgenville nursing home invited me to see their walls lined with paper hearts on Valentine's Day. Each heart was inscribed with a patient's name and their brief definition of love.

"Love is a bunch of kids," said Buck Skaggs.

"Love is God," said Tilly Schofner.

And 82-year-old Cassie Clay, who was sitting in her wheelchair near a window said, "Love is when you can't see the rest of your life without someone."

The love of her life, her husband Owen, had been gone 17 years. She'd loved him from the moment they met, and he was nicer to her than anyone she had ever known. Maybe he wasn't all that handsome to others, she said, but he was to her, and she could talk with him about anything. He usually gave her roses or candy on Valentine's Day, and she had saved the heart-shaped candy boxes and cards until she'd had to dispose of them when her property was sold at auction before she came to the nursing home a year earlier.

She wasn't there during the auction, but the day of the sale she felt the rest of her life was over. What she missed most were the items no one else wanted: the Valentine cards and those empty, heart-shaped candy boxes.

Just down the hall, 80-year-old Hascle Fancher, who had lost his wife, Juanita, in a fire at their farmhouse shortly before he came to the nursing home, summed up his definition of love with, "Love is all I got left."

I've saved a picture of 102-year-old Sedley and 98-year-old Bunnie Harreld of Ohio County, who were named "Mr. and Mrs. Valentine of 2002" at a Valentine's Day party in their honor at the Ohio County Senior Center. "Don't ever go to bed mad," Sedley advised.

He and Bunnie were married 80 years before they passed away within a few weeks of each other during spring of the following year.

A Marine's picture, page 92

III

Heroes

JULY 2012

Pathways of quiet patriots

Although 20 years have passed, I still remember the hint of a teardrop in Russell Hudson's eyes as his feeble hands lowered and folded the flag on the town square in Liberty.

At 86, he'd been raising and lowering the flag at the Casey County Courthouse, morning and night, for 21 years, without pay.

He'd been a bugler in the infantry during World War II. A childhood illness had damaged his eyesight so severely that he memorized the eye chart and lied about his age to get into the Army at age 17. The bugle on which he had played taps at hundreds of military funerals hung on his kitchen wall.

"I practice of a night here," he said. "But nobody hears me."

Hudson died several months after we met, but each year when I see Old Glory unfurled on July 4, I think of him and many other quiet patriots whose Kentucky pathways I have crossed over the years.

Walton Haddix of Clinton County has spent 12 years trying to persuade the Army that the late Lt. Garlin Murl Conner of Clinton County deserves a hearing to decide if he is eligible for the Medal of Honor for his remarkable heroism during World War II.

Conner's acts of courage in battle were discovered by Wisconsin Green Beret Richard Chilton, while Chilton was researching the war record of his uncle, who died in Conner's arms at Anzio beachhead.

In recent years Conner's commanding general, Maj. Gen. Lloyd Ramsey, and numerous others have pleaded, to no avail, with the Army Board for Military Corrections to consider new eyewitness evidence supporting Conner's eligibility for the Medal of Honor.

Ramsey has explained that in the heat of combat he neglected to recommend Conner for the medal at the time of his heroism. Haddix, a Navy veteran, is now working with a Lexington law firm to plead Conner's case in federal court.

If awarded the Medal of Honor, Conner would join the ranks of the most decorated soldiers of World War II—an honor now held by Audie Murphy, who served with Conner in the 3rd Infantry Division.

Then there is Eugenia Morrison, 83, of Barren County, who three years ago decided that something had to be done to reclaim the overgrown grave and surrounding cemetery where Revolutionary War soldier William Peers is buried in northern Barren County.

She enlisted the help of others and often spent her own money, clearing briars and other bramble from 30 gravesites, including the gravestone of Peers, who served at Valley Forge and fought in several Revolutionary War battles.

Community volunteers learned of her efforts and pitched in to help. The Disabled American Veterans erected a flagpole and flag. Now Morrison sees to it that the cemetery grounds are mowed and maintained.

She wonders who will look after the cemetery when she is gone.

And I am wondering who is left to follow the paths of Russell Hudson, Walton Haddix, Eugenia Morrison and many other Kentucky quiet patriots.

It is something to think about each time Old Glory is unfurled.

Editor's note: Conner was finally awarded the Medal of Honor in June 2018. Read more on page 82.

NOVEMBER 2012

Always room for one more

O n some Thanksgivings, Jerry Tucker and his late wife, Sandy, had as many as 125 of their children come home to South Fork Ridge for dinner.

The Tuckers are founders of Casey County's Galilean Home Ministries, a nonprofit organization that cares for children from all over the world who have been abused, neglected, rejected, or need medical treatment or a Christian education. They have adopted 30 children, and over the years taken in 800-1,000 other physically and emotionally impaired youngsters since their first adoptions of a boy, then two Sioux sisters three decades ago. They have two biological daughters.

The Tuckers moved to south-central Kentucky from Michigan in 1974—lured primarily by inexpensive farmland—and settled in Casey County, where a Mennonite community soon sprang up.

There they established a faith ministry that has grown with each child in need who has been brought to their door. Some are babies whose mothers are incarcerated. Many are from other countries and are victims of unspeakable cruelties.

A 10-year-old girl with disabilities from Guatemala had been sold by her mother at age 7 to an army camp, where she was held captive in a cave and abused by the soldiers.

A girl from Honduras had been severely wounded when gunmen murdered six members of her family, including her parents, when she was 4. Now 22, she attended Bible college, married, and is helping with babies at the Galilean Children's Home.

At age 12, Abdul Sammad from Afghanistan picked up what he thought was a toy beside the road in his war-torn homeland. It was a Russian roadside bomb that blew off both his hands, put out his left eye, and left him with other wounds. Assumed to be an orphan, he was sent to a refugee camp and eventually wound up at the Galilean Children's Home.

If you have visited the home's Bread of Life Café beside U.S. Highway 127 between Liberty and Dunnville, you may have seen him—the polite young man with no hands who buses tables.

What you may not know is that he became a proficient 3-point shooter on the Galilean Christian Academy's basketball team, was a top student in community college while earning an associate degree, and that he wants to re-enter college and study either pharmacy or business.

He has returned to Afghanistan twice for several months, located his mother, married a young woman there and has a 3-year-old son. He prays to bring his wife and baby to Kentucky.

Sandy Tucker, the woman who Galilean Children's Home's kids called "Mom," died in 2007 after a long battle with cancer.

"The last words she spoke to me on her deathbed were, 'Dad, don't quit. Don't ever give up,'" 72-year old Jerry Tucker says. "Those echo in my head all the time, especially when the economy gets tough as it has been the last three years."

Yet there is much to be thankful for this Thanksgiving at the Galilean Children's Home, where miracles happen each day, and where there always seems to be room for one more child.

JULY 2013

Never forgotten

Ever been in a restaurant when a total stranger picked up the dinner check for an old veteran seated nearby? If so, then maybe you've known one of those "July Fourth moments" when a random act of patriotism left you a little more red, white and blue.

Such a moment came for me when I learned that 74-year-old Margaret Creech Burkett of Paint Lick, a member of Inter-County Energy, has devoted the past eight years to a painstaking search for pictures and biographical notes of Garrard County's World War II veterans in order to preserve their memories in a book.

She's pored through hundreds of articles on microfilm, spent countless hours writing letters, made phone calls, traipsed through cemeteries and even traveled outside the state in search of information about old soldiers, sailors, airmen and Marines—most of whom she never knew. Along the way she endured two major surgeries and several months of chemotherapy, but never gave up.

When told she had stage 4 colon cancer, her first concern was that she would not be able to finish the book.

Her deepest regret is that she didn't start sooner, before so many World War II soldiers passed on.

No profit is involved. She will publish the book—*Never to Be Forgotten*—at her own expense and sell it at cost.

The more than 430-page typewritten manuscript, much of which she originally wrote in longhand (she doesn't own a computer), contains the names of nearly 1,500 of Garrard County's World War II service personnel, with information on some of them and pictures of nearly 900.

Some of them would not come home, most would never see their names or their pictures in a book, and several have been virtually forgotten—except by Margaret Burkett.

When Margaret was growing up on a farm near Lancaster, her father, Roy Creech, a Navy veteran, would not allow her to ride her pony on the road. But she often rode through her grandmother's farm to the Lancaster cemetery, where she visited the graves of military personnel whose pictures were on their markers.

Her family stopped in town to study the names of local servicemen on a large "memorial board" on the side of a store building. Special markings denoted those killed or missing in action.

"We were taught to respect the flag, we were taught to respect God and we were taught to respect the veterans that had fought for us so we could have freedom," she recalls.

Several years ago, Margaret assisted writer Rita Fox with research for a small book about Garrard County's WWII veterans, but there was not enough space to include them all. Hundreds more are included in her current work, but she is still searching for a number of veterans for whom she has names but nothing else.

Her hope is that others in her county and elsewhere around Kentucky will undertake similar projects as a tribute to veterans in Korea, Vietnam and more recent wars.

Thanks for the July Fourth moment, Margaret.

JUNE 2014

Let's remember the cost of freedom

Here they were in my hands, the most dangerous days of Dallas Jacobs' 91 years, scribbled in pencil on unlined paper in what he calls "kind of a diary" from World War II.

Reading over his entries I tried to imagine—but could not—what it must have felt like for him when, as a 20-year-old Lincoln County farm boy, he found himself behind two .50-caliber machine guns as the waist gunner on a B-17 bomber, flying 33 missions in the war-clouded skies over Germany and France.

After each mission, he recorded memories of what happened that day, and there was little chance that he could forget. He and his eight crewmates on the "flying fortress" were usually targets of heavy fire.

On one mission, only nine planes returned out of an 18-plane formation.

Once, their plane was so badly damaged by air and ground fire that, though it landed on a wing and a prayer, mechanics said they counted more than 600 holes in the aircraft, from as small as a pencil to several inches in diameter.

Jacobs was never wounded, but came close when the heel of his boot was struck by a piece of shrapnel.

"I don't know how we made it. I think the Lord was just watching over us. We did a whole lot of praying back in those days," says Jacobs, a longtime member of South Kentucky Rural Electric Cooperative.

Many of today's generation either aren't taught or don't bother to learn about

D-Day or Pearl Harbor, the Bataan Death March, Auschwitz or the Battle of the Bulge. Yet our freedom to ignore history has been bought at a dear price by countless thousands of veterans like Dallas Jacobs who laid their lives on the line, and by the many who paid in blood and never came home.

Part of Jacobs' entry from June 5, 1944, reads, "… Flak was intense and accurate … We saw plenty of boats in the channel today. They must be going to make a landing in France."

On June 6, history will mark the 70th anniversary of D-Day, when American and Allied troops did indeed storm ashore on the beaches at Normandy in the face of withering German fire from heavily fortified emplacements. Jacobs remembers peering down at the D-Day landing site through a haze of smoke on a bombing run near the coastline, and wondering how the troops would ever penetrate German defenses.

As war correspondent Ernie Pyle would write after the invasion, it seemed "a pure miracle." Jacobs writes: "I didn't know there was that many boats in the world."

Finally back at home in Kentucky, Jacobs married a pretty girl named Lillian Sanders. They had four children, nine grandchildren and 21 great-grandchildren. Dallas retired as a construction engineer with the state highway department. He lost Lillian in 2012.

Occasionally someone thanks Dallas Jacobs for what he did in World War II.

"It makes you feel good," he says.

NOVEMBER 2014

Great teachers inspire

When autumn whispers her last, sweet goodbyes, and November comes rustling over a leafy carpet of crimson and gold, I am often drawn back in thought to Elsie Butcher's fifth-grade classroom.

Even after all these years, the toasty, warm fragrance of freshly oiled pine floors and heat from the old steam radiators that hissed and clanged along the walls are as near as a chilly November morning.

Through many Thanksgivings since then, I don't believe I ever thanked Mrs. Butcher for making November and December such wonderful months for me in a school career that was thoroughly unremarkable.

I can hear and see her now through a haze of chalk-dust images on a gray November afternoon, resting against the front of her desk, arms crossed, cradling a book in her left hand as she read to us stories and poems of the season.

In some lost moment during one of those readings, it occurred to my wandering mind how perfectly words can paint a picture when properly arranged on paper. I liked the way words sounded when she read them.

Just now I am remembering her reading of James Whitcomb Riley's classic *When the Frost Is on the Punkin*, a class favorite, the second stanza of which I liked best:

They's something kindo' harty-like about the atmusfere

When the heat of summer's over and the coolin' fall is here—
Of course we miss the flowers, and the blossoms on the trees,
And the mumble of the hummin'-birds and buzzin' of the bees;
But the air's so appetizin' and the landscape through the haze
Of a crisp and sunny morning of the airly autumn days
Is a pictur' that no painter has the colorin' to mock—
When the frost is on the punkin and the fodder's in the shock.

Mrs. Butcher seemed to enjoy reading so much that I thought it must be great fun, and decided to check out a library book for myself. A new world of words and thoughts awaited in the works of Jim Kjelgaard, Montgomery Atwater and other fine writers of boys' outdoor adventure books—writers I might never have known had Mrs. Butcher not whetted my appetite for reading.

In high school English class several years later, most of my hours were spent gazing out the second-story window at a woodland in the distance—daydreaming about a future in forestry. But one day, as the class worked on an impromptu essay assignment, our teacher, the late Virginia Shaw, peered over my shoulder and whispered, "You can write."

It was news to me, and wasn't regarded with much importance at the time. But looking back, I realize that the seeds of imagination and fondness for words that Mrs. Butcher planted on that gray, November afternoon in fifth grade helped guide me into a lifelong career in writing.

Not long ago, I stopped by her home to say thank you—before another Thanksgiving passes.

FEBRUARY 2015

Hometown hero

Somewhere in the Washington County seat of Springfield should stand a statue of Louis Sansbury, who stood by the town when nearly everyone else fled.

The year was 1833 and an epidemic of Asiatic cholera was sweeping over much of Kentucky, killing thousands. An estimated one-tenth of the population died in Lexington, Russellville and Springfield, while many other communities suffered similar losses.

A Springfield newspaper reported that within 24 hours more than 100 people were stricken: "The deadly malady reached even the songbirds that fell lifeless from the great elm trees that shaded the farm yards and streets of the town."

Imagine Louis Sansbury's thoughts when nearly every able-bodied person in the town of 618 fled for their lives and left him to care for the sick and dying. He was 26 years old and the slave of a local hotel owner who, along with many other business people, gave him their keys as they left in panic.

What happened in the weeks that followed is the stuff of an epic novel that was never written.

Sansbury, along with a woman named Matilda Sims and a Presbyterian preacher named Cheeney, cared for the sick and buried the dead.

The story goes that Sansbury fed and cared for the bedridden with supplies taken from local stores. Though illiterate, he devised a method of markings to keep track of what he had taken so an accounting could be made when the merchants returned. Matilda cooked, and Louis carried food to the sick who were able to eat.

The *News Leader* newspaper in 1915 noted that he and Matilda prepared the dead for burial, and that Louis placed them in trenches he had dug on the outskirts of town.

Although he was hailed as a hero as the townspeople returned, one account said that Sansbury remained a slave until 1845, when grateful citizens purchased his freedom and set him up in business with a livery stable on Main Street.

In 1854, during another cholera outbreak, Sansbury again stayed behind to care for the sick and bury victims when many others left.

He died seven years later, presumably of natural causes, in the spring of 1861 at age 54, and was said to have been carried to his burial place "by the hands of those for whom he had risked his life."

Gus Cooper, a deacon at the predominantly black Holy Rosary Catholic church in Springfield, said he is hopeful that Sansbury, the first honoree of Springfield's annual African American Heritage Festival, begun in 2004, will one day be honored with a statue to safeguard his memory.

Though his grave is unmarked, he is remembered on two markers near the mass grave of 106 cholera victims in St. Rose Cemetery, and a framed painting depicting his heroism hangs at the Washington County Public Library.

Staff genealogist Linda Lawson says, "I doubt the people had any hint that an angel walked among them in the guise of Mr. Sansbury."

NOVEMBER 2015

What disability?

The 11-year-old Marion County sixth-grader whom I remember doing her homework from a wheelchair—with a pencil held between her teeth—is all grown up now.

Amanda Atwood turned 21 in August and is beginning her senior year at Campbellsville University. But she still completes some writing assignments holding a pencil in her teeth, or more often with a mouthpiece that enables her to type on a keyboard.

Since birth, Amanda has been virtually paralyzed from the neck down with arthrogryposis, a condition that prevents development of the joints and muscles.

Yet, from childhood, she has been determined not to let her disability deprive her of a meaningful life.

"I always tell people, 'I have a brain, and it functions perfectly.' As a kid, I didn't know as much about my disability, and I was scared about what people would think. But as I grew up, I realized it doesn't matter and I'm going to overcome anyway. My faith is a big part of the way I handle things."

She rejected the idea of being placed in a special-needs class in school and insisted on participating as best she could in PE classes; won a speaking contest as a member of her school's FFA chapter; and even made the cheerleading squad at Lebanon Middle School.

"I may not have the physical ability to do the moves, but I did the cheers as loud as I could, and that's what got me a spot on the squad."

She'd love to have played soccer or basketball, and she dreams of one day being able to camp out all night with other Big Blue fans at Rupp Arena, waiting for basketball tickets to the Kentucky Wildcats' annual Big Blue Madness.

Her parents, Anthony and Sandy Atwood—members of Inter-County Energy Cooperative—stay busy keeping up with Amanda's schedule. Her mother requested a move to third shift at her workplace so she'd be available to drive Amanda the 40-minute round-trip to college classes.

Amanda is in the Social Work Club at Campbellsville University, helps out with youth activities at her church and has donated 72 inches of her hair to Locks of Love.

"I would love to either work in rehab … or at something like a children's hospital. I just love kids," she says.

This month Amanda is a contestant in the Ms. Wheelchair Kentucky Pageant to be held in Louisville.

She never dreamed of being in the contest, until last year when she wrote a paper about spinal cord injuries for one of her classes and chose as her subject Casey Schaeffer of Green County, last year's Ms. Wheelchair Kentucky. Casey encouraged Amanda to enter the competition.

"I don't think my main goal is to win. I just hope I make an impression," Amanda says. "I feel like maybe I'm supposed to have a platform to reach other people, and that's why I chose social work as a career."

NOVEMBER 2016

Thanksgiving labor of love

November's convergence of two cherished American holidays—Veterans Day and Thanksgiving—calls to mind a Vietnam veteran and his wife who, through countless hours of volunteer service, have given many Kentucky veterans a special cause for thanksgiving.

Over the past 11 years, retired Army Sgt. Maj. James Gerald Vannoy, 75, and his wife, Phyllis, residents of rural Jessamine County and longtime members of Blue Grass Energy Cooperative, have presented service medals and ribbons to nearly 3,000 veterans from all branches of service, who never received, or have lost, their military medals and ribbons.

A shortage of metal for war supplies prevented some World War II soldiers from receiving their medals, while other medals were not authorized until after many soldiers were home from the war. The medal presentation ceremonies are held at the Thomson-Hood Veterans Center at Wilmore in Jessamine County.

One recent recipient was 90-year-old John B. Wheatley Jr. of Louisville, a World War II veteran who held back tears remembering the faces and gruesome images he witnessed when he and his fellow soldiers in the 42nd Infantry Division helped liberate the Nazi concentration camp at Dachau.

"On average we have 25 veterans that get their medals" at each presentation, Vannoy says. "We invite family members in, and it's usually overflow."

Veterans Center Activities Director Michelle Ewing notes the medal presentations are an important morale booster among the residents, and are memorable moments for their families. James Vannoy also assists veterans in several central Kentucky counties with getting their medals, and Phyllis helps with paperwork.

"Their dedication to making sure that veterans of the commonwealth are appropriately recognized ... is one of the most heartwarming experiences that I've ever seen," says Mark Bowman, executive director of the Kentucky Department of Veterans Affairs. "It's just amazing ... and they never want any praise."

James Vannoy grew up on a farm in Casey County, went into the Army at age 18 and served 30 years—including tours in Korea and Vietnam and three tours in Germany.

While working as a security officer at Thomson-Hood Veterans Center for several years after retirement from the Army, he got to know many of the residents and learned that a number had not received, or had misplaced, their medals and ribbons. So he began the necessary paperwork to acquire the medals. Now that he is retired, he and Phyllis continue the effort.

"The way I understand the regulation, each veteran is entitled to a free set of medals," Vannoy explains. "The average World War II veteran will get five to six medals, and some will get 10 or 12. About a year after this place opened, we had about 290 veterans, and 80% of those were World War II vets. Now, I think we have 69 World War II veterans left, and all of them are 90 or above."

"It's not work, it's a labor of love," Phyllis Vannoy insists of the couple's volunteer efforts. "You can't watch one of the ceremonies without shedding tears."

AUGUST 2017

Travelin' man

R oy Pullam's parents—who had little formal schooling—were determined that their children would get an education.

"I couldn't imagine myself being anything else but a teacher," remembers Pullam, one of six children in the family of a disabled western Kentucky coal miner.

He had plenty of time to imagine where life's highway might take him as he hitchhiked 37 miles each way from Providence in Webster County to Henderson Community College five days a week for two years in all kinds of weather.

During a snowstorm one night, when no one was on the roads, he nearly froze on the 9-mile walk from Dixon to Providence.

"The next morning I got up and said, 'Daddy, I don't think I can do this anymore.' And he said, 'Do you want to be like me?' I said, 'No sir.' He said, 'Well, you get out there and go.'"

Roy finished Henderson Community College, then earned a master's degree in history from Murray State University, with postgraduate studies at Indiana University and the University of Virginia.

Returning to Henderson as a teacher at Henderson's City High and North Junior High School, he and his students launched a project that would preserve a treasury of Kentucky history in words and pictures.

Realizing that many noteworthy citizens of the community had passed away without leaving a record of their life stories, Pullam organized his eighth- and ninth-grade students into a small video production unit he called Bonnet Productions, taken from letters in names of the students. Pullam's wife, Velma, often drove the bus on interview trips.

The project soon expanded far beyond Henderson County to all of Kentucky and part of southern Indiana. When it ended 26 years later with Pullam's retirement in 2006, more than 600 people had been interviewed: Holocaust survivors, statesmen, celebrities, sports heroes and hundreds of everyday folks whose life events left them with powerful stories.

Aiko Nakashima Allen of Henderson County described seeing the atomic bomb dropped on her native Nagasaki, Japan, in World War II. D.L. Ball of Webster County, a one-time acquaintance of Albert Einstein, shared memories of the great physicist.

Renowned heart surgery pioneer Dr. William DeVries, a fan of the Everly Brothers, said he played the Everlys' *Wake Up Little Susie* as patients were waking from anesthetics.

Today, most of Bonnet Production's interviews are on file at the Henderson County Public Library and at the University of Kentucky's Margaret I. King Library.

"One of my guiding principles was to let the kids see somebody that they could look up to and admire," Pullam reflects. Two days earlier, a young woman he had seen in Henderson said, "Mr. Pullam, you were my favorite teacher."

"When you're from across the tracks," he told me, "oh my goodness, when you get that esteem and appreciation, it's not anything you'd trade away."

NOVEMBER 2018

Medal of Honor

The official sounding voice of the woman on the phone asked Pauline Conner to please hold for a call "from the president of the United States."

You could have heard a pin drop in the Clinton County farmhouse in those seconds before President Donald Trump gave Conner the news she might have thought she'd never hear, that her late husband, Lt. Garlin Murl Conner, was at long last being awarded the nation's highest recognition for military valor—the Medal of Honor.

Pauline and the Conners' son, Paul, other family and friends were guests at the White House in June when Pauline accepted Lt. Conner's posthumous Medal of Honor. The discovery in military archives of three overlooked eyewitness accounts of Conner's World War II heroism had warranted an upgrade of the Distinguished Service Cross to the Medal of Honor, placing the Kentuckian among the most decorated soldiers of the war.

Conner died in 1998 at age 79. He had avoided talking about the war after returning to farm life in Clinton County, where he served as county Farm Bureau president for 17 years while voluntarily helping many Kentucky veterans obtain benefits. Pauline, a longtime member of South Kentucky RECC, still works part-time for the Clinton County Farm Bureau.

Her husband's remarkable story might never have been told had Richard Chilton, a Special Forces veteran from Wisconsin, not accidentally uncovered the Kentuckian's combat records while researching his own uncle's military history in 1996.

"I was just amazed at what I was looking at," he remembers.

Conner, who stood 5 feet, 5 inches and weighed about 120 pounds, had already been wounded in a previous battle when he slipped away from a field hospital to rejoin his 3rd Infantry unit on the German front in France in January 1945. In the face of a massive enemy troop and tank assault, he scrambled 400 yards unreeling telephone line in deep snow and, likely armed with a submachine gun, took cover in a 1 foot deep ditch for three hours as German troops, at times, advanced to within 5 yards. He finally called in artillery fire on his own position to save his unit.

Chilton tried unsuccessfully, beginning in 1999, to have Conner awarded the Medal of Honor, then was joined in 2000 by Navy veteran Walton Haddix of the Clinton County Historical Society—and their quest continued until 2018!

"It had to be done," says Haddix, a 50-year member of South Kentucky RECC. "As long as I had breath living, I was going to try to stay with it."

Chilton, 88, and Haddix, 81, both attended the White House Medal of Honor ceremony, along with many others who were among the dozens who had helped them along the way, and to whom they would likely have devoted this page if given the choice.

But surely most would agree that these two great veterans deserve special, stand-alone salutes for their relentless, two-decade pursuit of honor in Lt. Conner's behalf—and for reminding us all that it's never too late to do the right thing.

APRIL 2019

Old Friends

Long after they've outlived their usefulness for racing and breeding, many retired thoroughbred horses are finding their way to greener pastures at Old Friends Farm, a few bluegrass meadows southwest of Georgetown in Scott County.

Kentucky Derby and Preakness winners Silver Charm and War Emblem; Belmont winner Touch Gold; three-time Santa Anita Handicap winner Game On Dude; Breeder's Cup Classic winner Alphabet Soup; and one of Seabiscuit's movie doubles, Popcorn Deelites, are among the scores of thoroughbreds living storybook endings as they round life's far turn at Old Friends.

Ironically, Michael Blowen, the gentle man behind it all, had no interest in horses through most of his career. A longtime film critic for the *Boston Globe*, he was focused on stars of the silver screen. Then an editor invited him to an afternoon of racing at Suffolk Downs, where he "fell in love with everything."

He later apprenticed with a trainer at Suffolk and worked most of two years for no pay—mucking stalls, grooming and learning the finer points of caring for thoroughbreds.

"I got to the point where not only did I believe they were athletes, but I believed they were superior athletes to their human counterparts," he says.

During a visit to the Kentucky Horse Park while still with the *Boston Globe*, he'd been impressed by tourists waiting in line to glimpse retired racing legends Forego and Bold Forbes. And after taking a buyout from the *Globe* in 2001, while lamenting to a friend the sad fates of many famous thoroughbreds after their careers ended, he mentioned that he'd like to have a place for them to retire, where their admirers could feed them a carrot and get to know them beyond the numbers on a saddlecloth.

Chasing his dream turned out to be an endurance race. But finally, after much help from several believers—and a number of sympathetic skeptics—Michael and his wife, Diane White, who was also a popular columnist with the *Boston Globe*, were able to buy Dream Chase Farm in 2006 and transform it into a refuge for Old Friends.

Now, helped with donations from a long list of horse lovers and farm visitors, the Blowens and some 30 dedicated volunteers, including a few consumer-members of Blue Grass Energy, are caring for as many as 150 older thoroughbreds—from superstars to also-rans.

"We try to balance it out between famous horses and not-so-famous horses," Michael says.

Hall of Fame trainers and jockeys often show up at Old Friends to lend their support and to reunite with the horses who helped make them famous.

Michael glanced out the kitchen window of the farmhouse one afternoon and saw trainer Bob Baffert alone at the paddock, visiting his first Derby winner, Silver Charm.

"People say, 'This must be like your dream,' and I go, 'Are you kidding ... my real life's better than my dreams.'

"I never believed in my entire life that I would end up living in a house where I could look out my back window and see Silver Charm in my backyard."

AUGUST 2019

Still dancing

As a small child, Martha Sandefur often made her grand entrance into rooms at the family's Ohio County farm home with a flourish of little dance steps. It was as though happiness followed her from place to place.

"Martha, I hope you always dance," her father would tell her.

Indeed, life's dance went on and on for Martha Sandefur Tarry Simpson, who turned 105 in January.

She taught school for nearly three and a half decades—in Memphis, Tennessee, and in Kentucky's Marshall, Ohio and Henry counties, including Eminence Independent School.

University of Kentucky professor Dr. David Royse, one of her former Eminence High students, recalls that Martha never stopped sending him books to read.

"One impression that I have of her, that has kind of carried me through my career as an educator, is that she would pose a question about something that we'd had to read—*Don Quixote* or something—and if we hadn't done the reading, she would sigh…deeply. She never said anything that would humiliate you; it was just that sigh that you wanted to avoid hearing."

Widowed twice, Martha retired from teaching in 1978, which opened new chapters in her remarkable legacy. She spent several years helping edit a Henry County History, portrayed historic characters for various organizations, led church and civic groups and organized one of Henry County's benchmark events—the annual Henry County Pride in Arts Festival. Internationally acclaimed essayist Wendell Berry, mezzo-soprano Ilse Apestegui and operatic baritone Troy Cook are among the many who have been showcased at the festival.

When at age 97 Martha was presented Henry County's prestigious Patrick Henry Award for outstanding contributions to the community, a number of former students wrote to share memories of her influence.

"You showed me that a book could be my best friend; that a well-written story could take me places I could never find alone," one woman wrote. "I carry in the back of my mind an English teacher who planted love and appreciation of a whole world of art just by occasionally hanging a Renoir or Monet painting in our classroom."

Another noted that Martha had stayed in touch with many of her former students: "Still encouraging, still caring, still loving us as if we were still in that English room upstairs at the end of the hall. What an angel that God has allowed us to get to know and love."

Martha suffered a stroke in late 2018 that left her partially paralyzed on the right side, but left untouched her gift of speech, her marvelous mind and wonderful heart. She closed her eyes on a life well-lived one morning in May, surrounded by her loving family.

In her last days, perhaps she left us with a hint of how she planned to enter that ethereal doorway of eternity.

"Sometimes I watched her in her chair, or even in the bed, and I'd see her toes moving," her daughter, Gwen Nelson, told me. "She'd say, 'I'm still dancing.'"

Legacy of kindness

My most vivid memory of her is a sad one.

Margaret Ware Parrish was kneeling with tears in her eyes over the lifeless body of a cat that had been struck by a car in the middle of Midway's Main Street.

The cat didn't belong to her. In fact, it was a stray, one of the dozen or more homeless animals she fed just before dark every day during her rounds through the backstreets of the charming Woodford County village.

The retired Midway College physical education instructor was 77 at the time, but still climbing onto the hood of her 1992 Buick Century to leave food for a mother cat whose kittens were born on the porch roof of an abandoned house. Other cats appeared from alleys or from under old buildings as the Buick approached.

The feeding had begun some years earlier when a member of the city council, knowing Parrish's love for animals, told her about a cat that was starving in one of the town's back alleys.

Some people who didn't know her must have thought she was crazy, she told me, but she couldn't stand to see anything suffer or go hungry.

So, her historic home just outside of Midway had become a sanctuary for mistreated dogs and cats, an injured raccoon that a passerby brought to her door and the duck she had waded into a creek one cold night to rescue after it was attacked by dogs. She was caring for two dogs and 13 cats at home. The dogs rode with her during her evening cat-feeding rounds in town. When possible, she had homeless animals spayed or neutered in addition to having them treated for their injuries or diseases, all at her own expense.

Margaret Ware—she was never known as just Margaret Parrish—was something of a legend in Midway. She'd been a cheerleader for the 1937 state high school basketball champion Midway Blue Jays and, after graduating from Centre College, had returned to the community to teach at what now is Midway University. Popular Midway author Jonelle Fisher, in her *Morning's at Seven*, wrote that Parrish kept historical records of Midway, often flew a beautiful array of treasured kites and grew a prolific bed of evening primroses— inviting everyone in the community to watch them bloom just at twilight on midsummer evenings. She also organized Midway's May Day celebrations, complete with clowns, a Maypole and the crowning of a May Day Queen. But helpless birds and animals were her true passion.

When at age 91, Parrish passed away at her home in the early autumn of 2010, she left a generous bequest to the Woodford Humane Society. Townspeople adopted the animals that were then in her care.

Perhaps by fitting coincidence, her antebellum home, once a refuge for orphaned, sick and injured birds and animals, is now occupied by veterinarian Nancy McGregor's Midway Small Animal Clinic.

JULY 2020

Full circle

Some days at work, Erin Koke must think her life has come full circle. Born nearly three months early and diagnosed with cerebral palsy at age 2, she began treatment at Redwood, a not-for-profit therapy center near Fort Mitchell in Kenton County, which offers a wide range of therapeutic, educational and vocational services for several hundred children and adults with disabilities.

Over the next 17 years she and her parents, who live in nearby Cold Spring in Campbell County, made regular visits to Redwood for outpatient treatment of the deep muscle constrictions affecting primarily her legs and hips, and for therapy that helped her walk with forearm crutches. She later earned an associate degree in human services from Gateway Community College.

Today, at age 25, Erin is a fixture at the front desk of Redwood's welcome center. Hers is often the first face people see when they arrive, the last when they are leaving and the first voice they hear when they call. She was hired as afternoon receptionist at Redwood in 2019, and now makes the daily 15-minute bus ride to and from work at the facility, which serves an average of more than 500 clients.

"She's the perfect person to have at that front desk, not only because she has a great personality and she's really smart, but also because she has faced similar challenges to the people that we serve," says Brittney Burkholder, employment specialist. "You have to know a lot to do that job. You have to know everyone in the building and what they do, because a lot of people call and aren't clear who they need to talk to."

"She's been a godsend," adds Redwood Human Resources Generalist Maria Meade. "She is the most kind, caring person. The families have really gotten to know her. One day I had given her a little break, and while she was gone one of the parents walked in to get their kid and said, 'Oh…you're not Erin.' And they waited until she came back, because the little boy wanted to give her a hug before they left."

"I think the front desk fits my personality well, but I don't think I'm all that special," Erin insists, noting that it's possible her disability may be partially responsible for enhancing her people skills.

"Because I have a disability and people look at me more often—and ask me questions about it all the time—I need to explain to them, 'here's what it is, and here's how it affects me,' and I think that's brought my voice out more."

Then there are the little moments she takes home with her from work on some days, like the trusting smile that always warms her heart from a little boy named Logan.

Maybe in his eyes she sees herself as a child of 5 again, coming through those same doors that now have brought her full circle at Redwood.

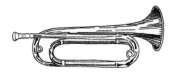

JULY 2022

A Marine's picture

One summer afternoon many years ago, on the porch of a farmhouse in Fleming County, Goldie Price showed me the picture of her son who was killed during World War II.

An antique frame held one of her most treasured keepsakes—the iconic photograph of six battle-weary Marines raising the flag atop an extinct volcano on the Japanese-held island of Iwo Jima. She'd been told that her son, Franklin Sousley, was the one with the rifle slung over his shoulder. His small portrait was inset in the top right corner of the picture that is commonly regarded as the best photograph of World War II.

Before Franklin shipped overseas on his 19th birthday, she'd told him, "Be careful son, and be good."

She said he wrote in his last letter home, "Watch the papers mom, they took a picture of us."

When the photo appeared in newspapers across the country, all the flag-raisers were ordered returned to the states to help promote national morale. But Sousley and two fellow flag-raisers were killed on Iwo Jima before the order reached them. Sousley was shot by a sniper.

Only in recent years has it been determined that he is not the Marine with the rifle on his shoulder in the photograph, but is instead the second Marine from the right whose facial profile is clearly visible.

"His daddy would've been proud," Goldie Price said. "He was about 9 years old when his daddy died."

Associated Press photographer Joe Rosenthal, who won a Pulitzer Prize for his photograph—and who took part in memorials honoring Sousley in Fleming County in 1975 and 1984—had inscribed Mrs. Price's picture at the bottom: "In tribute to the heroic actions of Pfc. Franklin R. Sousley, Co. E, 28th Division, 28th Regt. 5th Marine Div. on Iwo Jima."

The photograph and other Franklin Sousley artifacts are now in the care of Goldie Price's grandson, Dwayne Price of Ewing, a retired Maysville firefighter, former director of emergency management for Fleming County, and, like his late grandmother, a longtime consumer-member of Fleming-Mason Energy. Price was a primary consultant for Kentucky historian Ron Elliott's book, *From Hilltop to Mountaintop* (Acclaim Press), about the life and legacy of the Kentucky flag-raiser.

Before saying goodbye to Goldie Price on that long ago afternoon, I loaded my old Nikon and clicked a few black-and-white pictures of her holding the cherished photograph. No caption was needed for this picture, beyond what was written in the lines on her face.

She had lost one of Franklin's brothers with appendicitis at age 4, and another in a car accident at 18.

Her last years were spent with her son from a second marriage, and his wife, before she passed away in 1988 at age 83.

She had given up her original burial plot at the Elizaville Cemetery several years earlier to make space for a proper monument for Franklin. She was laid to rest on the hillside overlooking his gravesite.

Run for the marigolds, page 110

IV

Animals,
Nature and
the Outdoors

APRIL 2011

Hooked on river life

S pringtime always calls me back to a river.
The way I figure it, I may have been wandering Kentucky's stream banks since before I was born.

In the months before I came along, my mother often took long walks up the sycamore-shaded "creek road" that bordered our family farm on the Hanging Fork of Dix River in Lincoln County.

In those days, we lived just upstream from the site of the old Dawson's Mill, which had been dismantled years earlier. One of the heavy millstones served as a doorstep at our home when I was a boy.

Despite Hanging Fork's dark and mysterious name, it was a most peaceable and picturesque creek back then. It was even used in scenes of MGM's 1957 epic Civil War film, *Raintree County.*

Elizabeth Taylor and Montgomery Clift went wading not far from where I caught my first fish—a sun perch— with the help of my dad and a cane pole. We threw the sun perch back, but I was hooked for life.

In all the years since, Kentucky's creeks and rivers have never loosed their hold on me.

Each spring, I find my hip boots and wade into the Salt River upstream from Taylorsville Lake, at a place known as the Mill Hole. It is the site of another long-vanished gristmill on the edge of an old farm that I laid claim to several years back—mostly because the river runs through it.

I wanted my own creek road and sycamores, and I wanted those little gifts that a river can bring when it is on its best behavior.

Among the unusual walking sticks that have found their way home with me over the years is a favorite that I spotted on the river bottom in 3 feet of water one spring. A beaver had cut a slender, straight limb into a length of nearly 6 feet, then gnawed away every inch of the bark, leaving only hundreds of intricate tooth marks.

Another year, in a dead snag near the river, two baby pileated woodpeckers poked their heads from a hole in the trunk almost each time I passed. I finally realized they were mistaking my footsteps for the sound of their mother returning to the nest.

A few springs ago, while I was fishing in midstream above the Mill Hole, two Canada geese, which have nested for several years on a small island nearby, suddenly came riding the swift water down a stair-stepped riffle just upstream.

They did not seem to be trying to guide themselves, but were happily swirling and bobbing like toy rubber ducks that a child had tossed into the rapids. Once out of swift water, they lifted off, chattering past me on their way downriver.

But in no time they flew back upstream and, to my surprise, came floating, side by side, spinning and bobbing through the rapids once more. Maybe they'll be back again this spring.

MARCH 2012
The daffodil dance

If only the earth will feed us,
If only the wind be kind,
We blossom for those who need us,
The stragglers left behind.
—From Roadside Flowers *by Bliss Carman*

Those yellow flowers blooming in waves along the roadsides of Kentucky this time of year are known by several names—March flowers, March lilies, Easter flowers, jonquils, daffodils, narcissus and even buttercups.

Some of the names are technically incorrect, I know, including buttercups, which is what my family always called them. But so far there is no law against calling them whatever we like.

On a lonesome green knoll in a grove of black locusts near the heart of Kentucky, a multitude of yellow blossoms will soon begin their gentle dance into spring with no one there to see them. These flowers are all that remain to mark the spot my family once called home. We moved to another location on the farm, a half-mile away, when I was a toddler, and the old homeplace on the creek road is now barely a wisp of memory.

Virtually nothing is left there save the March flowers, which have bloomed in profusion every year despite repeated assaults by bulldozers, late freezes, droughts and flooding.

The house, barn and outbuildings, the orchard and its old-fashioned speckled apples that we once shook from the trees and remnants of the historic gristmill that stood along the nearby creek are all gone without a trace.

Yet these fragile yellow flowers greet the first breath of spring each year as though my family is still there, waiting to pick them for Sunday bouquets or hide Easter eggs among them for small hands to gather.

If you are thinking just now of the March flowers you have known, they may be calling you back to a place long ago and far away, beside a path or beyond a garden gate.

You may remember when, as a child, you discovered that by adding a bit of Easter egg coloring to the water of a vase holding jonquils, the flowers would absorb a thread of the color into the rims of their trumpets and petals, giving them a delicate red, blue or green outline.

Most of us in those days were blissfully unaware of the horticulturists' warning that daffodil sap has toxic properties, is dangerous if ingested and may cause skin irritations and itching if handled without gloves. Only recently did I learn this information on a computer—which thankfully had not been invented when I was a kid, and which often leaves me stranded these days beside life's cyber highway.

Just take it from one of the stragglers who's been left behind: if you've never stood knee-deep in memories and daffodils on a warm, soft day in March, you have missed a true moment of solitude, and maybe a rare chance for your soul to go dancing with spring.

MARCH 2014

Heifer with a heart

Someone could write a wonderful children's book about Miss Helen, the blind cow. All I can do is tell you about her heart.

One sweltering summer day in 2000, David Feldman of Garrard County found a baby calf only a few days old, lying in the weeds, either too weak or too afraid to move. Her mother had left her and was cooling off with other cows in a pond some distance away.

This calf had been born blind in both eyes.

She was of undistinguished Angus stock and black, except for a small band of almost white hair on her side that, to Feldman, resembled the irregular outline of a heart.

Many farmers who own sizeable herds of beef cattle might have allowed nature to take its course and left the helpless calf to die. But David, whose herd numbers about 100, cradled the baby calf in his arms and took her home to a stall in the horse barn, where he and his wife, Cindy, and daughter, Brandy, began bottle-feeding the animal that was to become a part of their family.

They named her Miss Helen in memory of Helen Keller, the renowned American author and lecturer who was both blind and deaf.

The Feldmans' Miss Helen was soon grazing in her own half-acre lot near the barn, where she quickly learned to find her way through the gate into a second pasture—and to the barn, water and feed troughs and elsewhere, as though she could see.

In the 13 years since she came to live with the Feldmans, her accidents have been mostly harmless brushes with gateposts or trees. She did step on one of her newborn calves a few years ago and broke one of its back legs, but the leg was placed in a cast, and soon the calf was romping in the pasture again.

Not only has Miss Helen given birth to several healthy calves, but she has raised orphaned calves and one set of orphaned twins, with a loving, gentle heart as though they were her own, says David, a member of Inter-County Energy Cooperative and owner of a lumber company in Lancaster.

"Seeing how she has endured all the things that have happened to her has been an inspiration," he says.

Last summer she was beset by a life-threatening health condition. A veterinarian examined a large tumor near her heart and treated her, but gave her only about one month to live.

But once again, Miss Helen, the blind cow with the large, imperfect, outline of a heart on her side, has defied the odds. Her tumor has shrunk to about a third of its earlier size, and she is still living happily in her little corner of the world—reminding us all of the words spoken by a wise woman many years ago: "Although the world is full of suffering, it is also full of the overcoming of it."—Helen Keller

APRIL 2014

Signs of spring

About this time each year—when the suddenly soft breezes stir among wildflowers and new grasses, Anthony Trammell's thoughts turn to the moon and signs of the zodiac.

Trammell, who lives in the Pine Knot community in McCreary County and is a member of South Kentucky RECC, "plants by the signs," as the saying goes.

He was once skeptical of the local old-timers' rigid insistence on planting by the signs, but trial and error changed his mind.

"I used to tell them the sign was right whenever the ground was," Trammell recalls.

But after a few mediocre crop yields in the garden and on the farm, each followed by reminders from his elders that he had planted in the wrong sign or the wrong moon phase, Trammell, 52, tried it their way, with some noticeable success.

He now plants corn when the moon is new, and plants root crops such as potatoes in the dark of the moon, or when it is waning.

"When you get the signs in the arms (Gemini, May 21-June 20) on the dark of the moon, it's time to wean calves. They won't bawl but just a day or two, and then they'll quit," he says.

Many such beliefs have been passed down mostly by word of mouth for generations, but *The Old Farmer's Almanac*, which dates to 1792, has been a benchmark reference for those who plant by the signs and the moon.

The almanac's original editor, Robert B. Thomas, suggested mowing bushes, and "killing them if you can," in the old moon (the last quarter until the new moon) when the "sign is in the heart" (Leo, July 23-August 22).

The 12 astrology signs and their coordinating dates can be found on zodiac charts in almanacs and often on planting calendars. Aries, the first sign of the zodiac, is attributed to the head, with the signs moving down the body, ending with Pisces at the feet.

Bennie Ray Bailey of Shelby County, a member of Shelby Energy Cooperative, was for many years the manager of a large farm supply store, and was a certified crop advisor.

He kept an *Old Farmer's Almanac* in his office to answer questions from farmers as to when the time was right for planting by the signs.

"I've seen enough of it to believe it's a sound practice, if you use common sense," says Bailey, 72.

He remembers that one of the busiest times of the year for seed sales at the farm supply store was during the dark of the moon in February, when farmers liked to sow clover and grass seed.

The popular early 1970s *Foxfire* book series (Anchor Press) spurred interest in the signs for a new generation.

"Planting is best done in the fruitful signs of Scorpio, Pisces, Taurus, or Cancer (when the signs are in the loins, feet, neck, or breast)," Foxfire sources advise. "Plow, till, and cultivate in Aries."

"Set fence posts in the old of the moon to prevent loosening."

And if you are not into farming and gardening, Foxfire also states that cutting your hair in Libra, Sagittarius, Aquarius or Pisces will make it grow stronger, thicker and more beautiful.

AUGUST 2014

A man of letters

He was a man after my own heart, Rob Wilson. Although we never met, I am guessing that his spirit must often amble along with me when I am wandering in the woods, drawn to curious formations of tree branches and roots, twisted by wind, water and time into shapes from A to Z.

Which brings me to the root of this story.

Wilson was born and died in Pickett County, Tennessee, but lived for several years in Clinton and Taylor counties in Kentucky. For many years he roamed the woodlands on each side of the border in search of white oak and hickory bark that he used to make chair bottoms and weave baskets.

The woodlands that he loved so dearly were to yield Rob Wilson a unique treasure.

Exactly when he first noticed a tree branch or root in the shape of a letter of the alphabet we do not know. Maybe it was an N or an F peeking from the limbs of a sassafras, ash or hickory, or a perfect S in the exposed root of a sycamore along a stream bank.

In any case, Wilson began searching for other, more complicated letters of the alphabet each time he ventured into the woods on foot. The project consumed much of his life.

He is said to have told the late Dr. Floyd Hay of Albany that he searched for the letter Q for seven years.

Finally, he had assembled all the letters in the alphabet, with duplicates of many, and the numerals 1 through 9. The letters were not carved, but a few were trimmed in a place or two.

Ironically, though Wilson was said to be unable to read or write, he dictated several booklets of poems and, with help, arranged his wooden alphabet into simple Scripture verses.

One of his granddaughters, Isabella Nicholas of Pickett County, Tennessee, remembers her grandfather in his later years as a tall man with a happy and contented disposition. He wore a felt hat and suspenders, played a banjo and sang. He died in 1973 at age 88.

"I never heard him say a bad word," she says.

The unusual alphabet was eventually bought by Hay, who displayed the collection in his office in Albany for several years. After Hay's death, his friend Dr. Steve Aaron, a prominent Louisville surgeon and Adair County native, acquired the alphabet and displayed it on boards at his home.

"It's art," Aaron once told me, "because it's the end product of some individual's creativity. Even though Rob was illiterate, letters were very important to him. You can look at them and see that a letter, to him, was just like a silver dollar."

A few years before his death, Aaron donated the collection to the Pickett County Public Library in Byrdstown, Tennessee, where it remains on permanent display, a remarkable legacy to an exceptional woodsman: a man of letters.

JANUARY 2015

Icy wonders

"**S**imply for the beauty of it."

Tom Martin answers without hesitation when asked what so often draws him outdoors during Kentucky's worst winter weather.

An author, photographer and authority on the sport of rappelling, Tom recalls the severe winter of 1977 as the year he began his cold pursuit of beauty.

Snow and ice had brought much of Kentucky to a standstill that January, and Tom was visiting a friend in a local hospital when he overheard a woman tell of seeing hollow disks of snow in fields, which she said resembled doughnuts standing on edge.

Tom drove out with his camera to have a look and, sure enough, began seeing them by the dozens. Never had he seen anything like them, and hasn't seen them since. They varied in diameter from 6 inches in some locations to a foot or more on hillsides near Camargo in Montgomery County.

Warmer temperatures the day before and extreme cold that night had apparently produced a layer of snow of the perfect consistency that a strong wind had rolled it into hollow tubes, many of which were left standing upright like big white doughnuts.

"For many days in early 1977, all I did was explore God's beautiful world," Tom says.

Sometimes accompanied by a friend, but often alone, he searched hills, creeks and cliffs in parts of Montgomery, Wolfe, Menifee, Powell, Lee and Estill counties, and was amazed at what he found.

Waterfalls 60 feet high were transformed into pillars of ice, as though the cascading stream had stopped in midflow. Young hemlocks and pines were suddenly snow sculptures, and a dainty, frozen prism of light had become, for a few grand hours, the centerpiece of a rock shelter.

In a Wolfe County cave, stalagmites of ice, known as hydromites, had formed when drops of water from the cave ceiling froze on the colder cavern floor, creating graceful, crystalline columns. Tom found in a Lee County cave a forest of hydromites—many of them more than 7 feet tall—extending more than 100 feet into the cave from its entrance.

It was, he would write, like being transported to another planet where delicate columns of ice seemed like crystal buildings in a crystal city. Standing alone in the garden of ice—amid silence, except for the dripping of water from the cave ceiling—he was moved to tears by the beauty of the place.

His search for such sights continued during the severe winter of 1978-79, and he included many of his photos in a book called *Kentucky Ice: A Winter Adventure*. Although conditions for such phenomena have rarely occurred as dramatically in Kentucky since then, he still goes looking for hidden beauty each time winter turns ugly.

If you try it yourself, Tom cautions, be careful of falling ice. Oh yes, and he wrecked his car twice on those early trips.

MARCH 2016

See the forest for the trees

One of my favorite hiding places as a kid was in a hollow sycamore tree beside a small stream meandering through the woods on the Lincoln County farm where I grew up.

I thought the old sycamore was a giant back then, but it was a mere sapling compared with the massive sycamore in Montgomery County—with a girth of more than 35 feet—that is the former state and national champion or the current state champion in Clark County, which is more than 26 feet around and more than 116 feet tall.

Diana Olszowy, who recently retired from the Kentucky Division of Forestry, kept track of Kentucky's champion big trees and some of their interesting stories.

The big sassafras tree that stands beside South Fredericka Street in Owensboro is not only the National Champion sassafras—at 23.1 feet in circumference and 58 feet tall, it's the largest known sassafras in the world. It narrowly escaped a bulldozer's blade back in 1957 when the street was being widened.

Its owner at the time, Grace Rash, stood her ground with a shotgun until the governor's office directed that the tree be spared. It is today a historic landmark.

With Kentucky losing its forest lands at what some scientists estimate is well over 100 acres a day—much of it to development—the American Forests Champion Trees national register and the Kentucky Division of Forestry's Champion Trees program are helping raise public awareness of our forest heritage and the need for increased commitment to forest stewardship.

The list of Kentucky Champion Trees now numbers 96 species, 10 of which are also National Champions. They are: American basswood, Fayette County; blue ash, Jefferson; chinkapin oak, Harrison; Fraser magnolia, Harlan; pignut hickory, Allen; river birch, Perry; sassafras, Daviess; shellbark hickory, Greenup; shumard oak, Powell; and slippery elm, Jefferson.

Olszowy notes that a former National Champion bur oak in Bourbon County, which was recently damaged by wind and lost its title, was already a small tree when the Mayflower landed.

If you find a big tree that you believe may be worthy of nomination as a state or national champion, you can check existing records for Kentucky's champion big trees by contacting your local forester or calling the Kentucky Division of Forestry.

Measurements of circumference are taken 4 1/2 feet from the ground, and the Division of Forestry has some simple methods for calculating the height and crown spread measurements.

Some non-native species, such as the ginkgo, are not eligible for state competition, but can be nominated as national champions.

The ginkgo is widely believed to have been brought to Kentucky by famous statesman Henry Clay, who acquired a few seedlings from Japan in the mid-1800s.

Two ginkgo trees said to be traceable to Clay still survive. One is in Frankfort, the other in Breckinridge County.

Maybe someone knows where there is another.

APRIL 2016

Run for the marigolds

While many thoroughbreds fantasize about running for the roses this time of year, a Woodford County miniature donkey named Justin dreams only of munching marigolds.

The fact is, Justin has been living in a virtual bed of roses since he was knee-high—and he's now barely 3 feet tall.

You see, Justin is best friends with someone his thoroughbred cousins often spend their racing careers in search of—Lady Luck.

It all began more than two decades ago when he came to live in the Connecticut stable of a kindly woman named Barbara. She eventually bought a farm in southern Woodford County and moved to Kentucky with a few horses, along with Justin and another miniature donkey named Chester, who died in 2011.

When Barbara passed away about a year later, she left in her will a sizeable trust fund for Justin so that he would be lovingly cared for the rest of his life. He now lives at the farm next door, which is owned by Barbara's friends, George and Kathy Smock. A check arrives each month from the trust manager in New York to pay Justin's expenses.

"He has the run of the farm," George says. "He spends the night in the barn, then during the day he's just loose and goes anywhere he wants. He goes up to the house and is kind of hard on my wife's flowers, because there are certain flowers he will eat; marigolds are a favorite."

How Justin developed a taste for flowers is not known, but it was obvious from his weight that he'd been eating nearly anything he wanted while in Barbara's care.

"She was killing him with kindness," George insists. "The first thing we did was put him on the Jenny Craig plan and got him to lose a lot of weight."

Diet notwithstanding, Justin still enjoys between-meal snacks at the bird feeders, in the flower garden and by scavenging through the empty stalls of the big horses boarded at the farm. Like a vacuum cleaner with long ears, he goes from stall to stall, cleaning up leftovers in the feedboxes after they are turned out in the morning.

Justin is missing a couple of molars, making it necessary for George and Kathy to brush his teeth about once a week, in addition to his patting and grooming.

Farm visitors sometimes find him lying in the driveway where he often likes to rest. And when horses on the farm are kicking up their heels this time of year, Justin rarely breaks into so much as a trot—unless he is caught in the pasture by a spring shower, or hears the feed room door open.

No, you'll never see Justin in a race, but I'll bet he'd like to be there when some high-stepping thoroughbred is fitted with the garland of roses at this year's Kentucky Derby.

Those roses would be great for snacks, until the marigolds bloom.

JULY 2016

The peace of purple

On the wings of a boyhood memory, Dan Crowe can still see his father, Robert, sitting in the yard of their Spencer County farmhouse in the hush of a summer evening, watching purple martins chase after flying insects along nearby Simpson Creek.

"Every night after supper he'd sit out there," Dan recalls. "I thought that was kind of odd. I didn't know how Dad could sit there that long and watch birds."

But if, as a philosopher once put it, life can only be understood backward, then Dan's understanding of his father's armchair visits with purple martins was still many years away.

Dan did put up a martin house or two after he was grown and living in Taylorsville, where he worked for the water company. A few birds occasionally showed up for a brief visit, but none ever stayed, and Dan finally gave up.

More than 30 years passed before Dan retired and moved with his wife, Marcia, to a home in the country near the Spencer County community of Elk Creek. There was plenty of open space for martin houses.

Four birds showed up the first year, but three of them starved during a cold, rainy spell that lasted several days, when there weren't enough flying insects to keep them fed.

In an effort to save the last bird, Dan bought crickets and flipped them high into the air with a plastic spoon within a few feet of the hungry female—a feeding method he learned from the Purple Martin Society website.

It took the bird a while to catch on, but after she finally swooped down to catch one of the crickets, "She didn't miss," Dan remembers.

He now has 40 nesting boxes—made to resemble gourd birdhouses—in which he hopes more than 150 young purple martins will hatch this year. Marcia keeps track of how many babies leave the nests; 96 last year.

Each martin house has an entrance that is 1 3/8 inches in height, just large enough for purple martins to enter, but designed to keep out predator birds.

Not only do many birds return to Dan's colony after wintering in South America, but Dan is almost certain that some, even most, return to the same houses. The first bird appeared back at his colony this year on March 1.

Dan is there to welcome them with crickets when the weather is cold, and on quiet summer evenings, like his father those many years ago, he can be found in a chair, just watching the birds chase after mosquitos and other insects.

"Only I sit there longer than he did, and I pull my chair up closer," Dan says. "And I'm thinking, 'Wow, now I know where he was. I know his frame of mind.'

"It's like sitting around a campfire, or listening to water in a stream. It has a real calming effect on you."

SEPTEMBER 2016

The majesty of monarchs

On the soft, dying breath of summer, about this time each year, there flutters past me a monarch butterfly wearing wings of autumn orange interlaced with dark bands—as pretty as a maple leaf in late October, or an exquisite sliver of stained glass come to life.

Some days I may notice several that appear to be drowsily on their way to nowhere, but in fact are on a general southwesterly heading to a very special place, far away, that they have never seen.

If they make it, they will join millions of others to overwinter in a remote pine and fir forest high in the Sierra Madres of central Mexico. Often, there are tens of thousands covering a single tree.

The fall migration of monarchs through Kentucky invites us all on nature's fascinating flight of fancy.

Some years ago, when I noticed monarchs clinging to milkweed blossoms on my little remnant of farmland along Salt River, I decided to mow around the patch of milkweeds and leave it for the butterflies.

To my surprise, many others have had the same idea on a much grander scale.

Sunni Carr, a biologist with the Kentucky Department of Fish and Wildlife Resources, chairs a steering committee representing many individuals, organizations and agencies—from garden clubs to school groups—that are dedicated to providing suitable habitat for monarch stopover sites during their migrations.

Milkweeds on the Kentucky landscape are critically important in the life cycle of the monarch, which both lays eggs and feeds on milkweed. It is an especially important food source for the monarchs we see at this time of year, which are likely part of the "fifth generation" making the long flight to overwinter in Mexico before coming out of the forest months later to lay eggs and start the life cycle again.

"So no monarch that goes to Mexico ever traverses up through North America and then back down," says Carr. "What we've learned is that the biggest limiting factor when they're up in North America is, we need to make sure that those food plants are there that they need to complete their life cycle—flowering plants, even flowering trees and shrubs, are extremely important. And they *have* to have the milkweed."

Swamp milkweed is a monarch favorite, but there are dozens of other suitable types available from a number of nurseries.

A storm in Mexico last year is believed to have depleted the monarch population by about 50%, and the U.S. Fish and Wildlife Service has been petitioned to declare the monarch a threatened species.

We can help restore the population by leaving some milkweeds and other flowering plants when we mow, or by joining the effort to plant way stations for monarchs.

For more information, contact your local garden club or Cooperative Extension agent, or write to: Kentucky Department of Fish & Wildlife Resources, 1 Sportsman's Lane, Frankfort, Kentucky, 40601.

JANUARY 2017

A forest of monuments

The way I figure it, Floyd Wells squeezed every last ounce of life out of 92 years.

When I last saw him, on a warm autumn afternoon in 1985, he was planting walnut tree seedlings on a hillside above his place along Polls Creek in Leslie County.

How was it, I wondered, that a man of 91 could find such obvious satisfaction in planting trees that he might never live to see grow beyond knee-high?

Yet Floyd could see a forest in the seedlings, and the thought of it brought him a measure of the joy he had known as a boy, wandering through a towering expanse of virgin timber that stood on this land before it was logged in the 1930s.

He had long ago begun planting seedlings to replace the trees that had been harvested, and he guessed that by the time we met he had planted more than 250,000.

In the meantime, he had operated a country store, which eventually grew into a small chain of four stores. He'd been a postmaster, a sawmill operator, worked on the railroad, taught school for a while and farmed, among other things. When many of his neighbors sold out and moved north to find work during the 1940s, Floyd bought much of their land.

He ordered hundreds of peach trees and developed an orchard and cannery that survived for a few years. All went pretty well with the cannery, except when a few cannery workers began sampling the fermented juice from the peelings that had been disposed of in barrels that caught rainwater.

Later, he decided to start a chicken cannery. But two weeks after storing many cans in the basement, he heard what sounded like a shotgun blast. Several of the cans of chicken had spoiled and were exploding—scattering their foul-smelling contents all over the basement.

Floyd often laughed until he cried remembering such stories.

He and a neighbor tapped sugar maple trees and left the sap in a large kettle to be cooked down into syrup the next morning. But a neighbor's bull came by during the night and drank the kettle dry.

Then there was the time one of the local roughnecks tried to fly, jumping off a cliff while flapping two large turkey wings. He lived, but never flew again.

Floyd was born in the spring of 1894 on the banks of Bear Branch in Leslie County, and was buried there on a spring day in 1987. His heart gave out while he was cleaning around his walnut trees, and he died at a hospital soon afterward.

But all those trees he planted and nurtured until he died are now a forest of monuments to his love of nature and his heart for conservation. His children now manage some 7,000 acres of Leslie and Perry county timber and mineral resources known as Floyd Wells Coal & Land Company.

What a life!

MAY 2017

Kentucky bird man

Visitors to the Jefferson County farm home of Brainard Palmer-Ball Jr. sometimes ask why he has left, undisturbed, a patch of blackberry brambles in the front yard.

His answer: "The indigo bunting nests there every year."

"That's all we can do, as individuals, is affect a little bit," he says. "When you've grown to know birds and wildlife, you learn what they use. Then you can appreciate that little patch of ragweed or that section of hedgerows that you don't completely clean up with weedkillers."

Palmer-Ball has certainly grown to know birds, perhaps as well as anyone in Kentucky. *The Kentucky Breeding Bird Atlas* and the *Annotated Checklist of the Birds of Kentucky* are among the markers of his successful career as a terrestrial biologist, a career that began on the 300-acre family farm where he grew up and to which he is now retired at age 59.

As a youngster, he was mildly interested in the birds gathered around the feeders that his late mother and father kept stocked in the backyard. But it was while wandering along one of the paths on the farm one day at age 14 that he saw, perched on barbed wire, a bird that gave wings to his calling in life.

"I didn't recognize it, but I looked it up and figured out it was an Eastern kingbird," he remembers.

From then on, he was hooked.

After completing his master's degree studies at the University of Louisville, he joined the Kentucky State Nature Preserves Commission as a zoologist and would spend the next 24 years, as he once said, studying "anything in my path that flowers, flies, swims or sings."

Of the 380 species of birds known to inhabit Kentucky, he has seen approximately 360 firsthand—and can identify most by their call or song. Yet there are some occasional surprises, such as the little stint, a shorebird from Asia rarely seen in the U.S.—and even then usually on the Pacific Coast—that he observed at a flood retention basin 10 years ago in Louisville.

Curiously, he has noticed that some birds once rare in Kentucky, such as the blue grosbeak and tree swallow, have now become fairly common, while others, including Bewick's wren and Bachman's sparrow, both rather common in the mid-20th century, have now essentially disappeared. Several pairs of ravens have taken up permanent residence in a few southeastern Kentucky counties, while the bobwhite quail population continues a notable decline, due to loss of suitable habitat and perhaps more predation.

Palmer-Ball believes landowners are the most critical partners in protecting threatened plants and animals, many of which are on private land.

In an article for *Land, Air & Water* magazine some years ago, he wrote, "If I've realized one thing in all my years, it is that significant contributions to biodiversity conservation can come from seemingly the most insignificant of actions."

Which brings us back to that patch of blackberry briars left undisturbed in his front yard.

JULY 2017

An ode to Otis

Somewhere on the list of dog heroes there must be room for Otis.

He was just an average dog on the outside, of medium build and mixed border collie ancestry. But on the inside, behind his big brown eyes, under his brown and white coat, there must have been a heart the size of his dog dish.

His owner, Byron Coffman, a Richmond firefighter and Casey County EMT, remembers that when Otis was happy his tail wagged so wildly that it almost appeared to be rotating, as if he might lift off at any moment.

Coffman's wife, Angie, and their children, Jenna and Harper, got Otis from some friends when he was a puppy and brought him home to their farm in the Bethel Ridge community of southeastern Casey County. His comical unsteadiness as a small puppy earned him the name Otis, after the lovable but seldom sober Otis Campbell on the old *Andy Griffith Show*.

Otis was an outside dog from the start and, once grown, was allowed to roam the farm fields. He was soon spending a good bit of time away from home, and one day Coffman saw him chasing cattle on the farm next door.

He gave Otis a stern lecture, brought him home, and told the neighboring landowner, his friend Mike Woodrum, that if Otis had gotten in the habit of chasing cattle, something would have to be done.

That is when he learned from Woodrum, a Kentucky state trooper, that Otis had adopted a crippled young heifer in Woodrum's beef cattle herd, and that the only time he ever chased cattle was when they were threatening to mistreat the heifer that had been born with a twisted front leg.

Over the next three years, regardless of the weather, except for coming home to eat, Otis spent virtually all his time with the crippled Charolais heifer, usually no farther away than 15 to 20 feet, whether she was grazing or resting.

Neither Coffman nor Woodrum, both members of South Kentucky RECC, could come up with an explanation of why Otis took it upon himself—with no training—to protect the crippled cow with such dedication. But there was no doubt that, of the approximately 30 head of cattle in the herd and four horses in the field, he had chosen to befriend the one with the crippled leg.

Then, back in the spring, Otis went missing for four days, and Coffman and Woodrum got concerned. Woodrum finally found him in a wooded hollow on the edge of the pasture—he was dead.

There was no sign of a struggle, or a fight with coyotes, nothing to indicate that he had been injured in any way. It was as though he had simply lain down to rest.

I wish the story had a happy ending. But I thought you ought to know that Kentucky lost a mighty good dog … and a crippled cow lost the best friend she ever had.

JUNE 2018

Bluebells and pawpaws

A rite of spring for me each year is traipsing along the remnant of an old wagon road to all that's left of what once was someone's farm beside the river.

My name may be on the deed, but the place of just under 30 acres "more or less" doesn't really belong to me. It belongs mostly to the Salt River that divides it nearly in half, and to the trees, fallen logs, wildflowers, birds and animals that have taken control since a long-ago family gave up farming there. All that is left of their passing is a crumbling section of stone fence, an abandoned tobacco barn, some lonely daffodils and the initials that two unknown sweethearts carved on a beech tree.

Nature has reclaimed this place to suit itself, never bothering to discuss it with me, or even to acknowledge my occasional visits. And nature is proving to be a better caretaker than I have been.

One spring some years back, I noticed a few scattered clumps of bluebells blooming on a wooded slope just below the road. The next spring there were more, and the next even more, until now they bloom in profusion along a stretch of maybe 30 yards below the road.

Where they came from I don't know. I have been up and down the river on foot for several miles over the years and scarcely remember ever seeing a bluebell, much less a natural garden of them that gets bigger each spring.

A small forest of pawpaw trees—maybe more than a hundred—has taken root along 50 yards of the road. There must be something about the forest floor, the sunlight and north-facing slope in that one spot below the river bluff that makes everything just right for bluebells and pawpaws.

Finally, under the hood of my old tractor inside the weathered barn, I am greeted most every spring in recent years by a field mouse that scurries from a cozy nest in the space between the grill and the radiator, jumps onto an axle and vanishes into some bales of straw.

Her nest is usually a bit larger than a softball. It is made of bits of grass, what looks like stuffing from a cushion, and almost always at the heart of the nest, some soft moss and one tiny bit of bright red cloth. The first time I saw it, I thought the little fragment of crimson cloth must have been an accidental find. But I dispose of the nest each year before starting the tractor, and a new bit of the same red cloth appears the next spring. I can't imagine where she finds it, or even that she is the same mouse.

It is a puzzle to ponder walking back to my truck on the old wagon road, leaving behind the river, the bluebells, pawpaw trees and a field mouse with an eye for decorating—on that little clump of earth that now is more theirs than mine.

MARCH 2019

Susan the gardener

Growing up on the family farm in rural Wayne County, Susan Hutchinson Miller never imagined that the chores she disliked so much as a girl would today be one of her driving passions.

A fifth-generation farmer, she remembers how she, her two sisters and three brothers worked planting and picking tomatoes, cucumbers and peppers that her late father, Ray Hutchinson, grew on contract with canning companies on their 40-acre farm in the Frazier community.

"We had to work," she says. "We didn't have a choice. As kids we didn't like it ... but whether you were cooking or working in the fields, everyone did something."

Now, at age 50, Miller looks back on those formative years as a fitting prelude to what has grown into a profitable and rewarding business for her family.

She and her husband, George, and their two daughters, Kanesha, 21, and Allison, 19, are residents of Lincoln County, where the vegetables from their gardening and high tunnel/greenhouse business are popular staples at the farmers market, at some local restaurants and produce auctions and at a roadside produce stand they operate in the warm months in front of their home on State Route 78 just west of Stanford. Susan raises bees for both honey and pollination of her vegetable crops.

George is employed by a manufacturing company in Danville, while Susan also serves as the family resource center coordinator for the backpack program and other services at Stanford Elementary School. Both devote many hours to their produce business and to helping others, including donations of excess produce. Susan has started a school garden at the elementary school and is organizing a small greenhouse project for schoolchildren through which the vegetables would be delivered to elderly residents in the community.

The Millers were honored in 2015 as Small Farm Family of the Year at Kentucky State University's annual Small Farm Conference. And when they hosted a farm-to-table dinner at their place last summer, more than 50 guests showed up from as far away as Bowling Green and Louisville to enjoy the food and learn some of the secrets of the Millers' success—which Susan says all trace back to the gardening skills passed down through her family and the lessons about hard work she learned in her youth.

Nearly every Sunday, Susan and her family still travel back to Wayne County for church and dinner with her mother, Zelma, a longtime member of South Kentucky RECC, and with many of her siblings and their families at the farm where it all began.

Now, Susan is passing along many of her parents' lessons to her daughters.

"My dad used to tell us, 'If I'd had the opportunities you kids have, the sky would be the limit.'"

She's hoping that, although neither of her daughters has shown much interest in farming so far, at least one of them, after college, may grow to love it as she has, and carry the family's farming tradition into yet another generation.

MAY 2019

A's and bees

As a youngster back in Martin County, growing up near the waters of Emily, Beauty and Lovely creeks, Lloyd Sartin often went with his father into the woods in search of "bee trees" from which they gathered honey and relocated swarms of wild honeybees from the woodlands to their own hives.

Now, many years later, Sartin, a consumer-member of Fleming-Mason Energy Cooperative and an alternative middle school teacher at Rowan County's Bluegrass Discovery Academy in Morehead, is sharing with students the beekeeping skills from his past through a course in which they're learning the essentials of beekeeping.

He sees the art and science of beekeeping as both a valuable green project and a cultural connection for the students, some of whose ancestors kept honeybees. Approximately 50 students have been involved in the course since it began in 2017. Some of them helped choose its name—the BeeGood Project.

While Schools Superintendent John Maxey and Principal Jay Padula both liked the idea of a beekeeping class and considered it a win-win for students and the environment, Sartin says there were obvious early concerns relating to safety for students and the placement of beehives a safe distance from school. Students take turns wearing protective suits to check the hives, which are located near a wetland where fruit trees have been planted about 2 miles from the school.

"They really enjoy it," says Sartin. "I'm sure it's got something to do with the fact they're getting outside the classroom. But at the same time, they are learning."

Currently, the class has four hives, including one that is left empty in case someone calls with a wild swarm of bees that can be given a new home in the BeeGood Project apiary. One such swarm has already been relocated.

Support for the project has become truly a community affair. School bus driver Larry Hood, a longtime beekeeper and consumer-member of Clark Energy Cooperative, has joined Sartin as a mentor for students, helping them build beehives and learn the importance of maintaining the health of honeybees.

Citizens Bank and the Morehead State University Art Department helped paint the hives with decorative designs. Grants secured through the nonprofit UNITE Coalition and Rowan County Middle School Youth Services Center were used to purchase fruit trees, fertilizer and beekeeping supplies. Owners of the local Honey & Bee Connection and a member of the Rowan County Schools Transportation Department donated protective beekeeper suits and hats.

Class member Hagan Hayes, 14, remembers that before his dad died, his family had a couple of hives of bees. He thinks his dad would like knowing he's studying beekeeping and hopes to have some hives of his own one day.

Makayla Robinson, 15, and Brooklyn Eldridge, 14, have been surprised at what they've learned about beekeeping and honey production.

"When I get older, I'm going to have bees myself," Makayla says. "I think more people should actually look into it."

Lloyd Sartin likes that.

Lost lore

A fellow reporter at the newspaper where I worked years ago asked if I'd ever met Nevyle Shackelford in Lee County

I had not.

"You really need to meet him," the reporter said, easing into a story of the snowy winter day when he and "Shack"—as he was known to his friends— were in the woods.

As they walked along a trail the reporter said Shackelford told him, "a red fox is following us, watching us from up on that ridge."

My friend turned, scanned the ridgeline and saw nothing. But when they followed the ridgeline on their return, there in the snow, he said, were fresh tracks of the fox that had been watching them, just as Shackelford had told him.

I got to know Shackelford in the years that followed. He was simply a human library on matters of Kentucky's flora, fauna and folklore. So good, in fact, that the University of Kentucky College of Agriculture hired him for several years to write a monthly page called *Outdoor Lore*, which was circulated to media around the state.

His subjects covered everything from wild plants used as food and medicine, to superstitions, ghost tales and myriad other fascinating lore.

He wrote of "water witches" who use the forked branches of certain trees to locate underground streams; of corn shocks in autumn, the beauty of winter, the nitrogen benefits of lightning, of spider webs, wildflowers and the demise of whippoorwills and bobwhite quail.

"I like all birds very much, but come right down to the nitty-gritty, I think my favorite is that wee animated bunch of feathers that calls itself the chickadee."

After gaining the confidence of chickadees around his place near Beattyville, he said he finally could call a flock of them from the woods and feed some birds from his hand. A few would even try to follow him into the house.

The barn swallow was another bird that liked being around people, he wrote, and he told about a game that he had watched them play in flight.

"I have seen these birds play for hours with a feather. One bird would get a feather in its beak, soar high into the sky, release the feather and then the whole flock would dive for it as it fell. The swallow getting the feather would fly high … and repeat the performance. I have seen them do this with a leaf and string."

He insisted that a pileated woodpecker hammers a dead tree 12 times—"no more, no less"—with each volley of pecks. I've never counted to see if he was right.

In his golden years he wrote poetically of the weather phenomenon known as Indian summer—that halcyon time of autumn marked by a brief spell of warm, hazy, summer-like days, which often occurs in November.

My friend Nevyle Shackelford died in the spring of 1999 at the age of 89, leaving a blank space in Kentucky's outdoors as lonesome as the call of the whippoorwill.

JUNE 2020

Miracles on the wing

A few of the pigeons you see flying just above the treetops as you travel the highways may be equipped with more sophisticated guidance systems than your expensive GPS device—if they're homing pigeons.

Given the birds' intelligence and amazing sense of direction, it is little wonder that naturalist Charles Darwin and inventive genius Nikola Tesla were fascinated with pigeons.

My appreciation for the species took wings many years ago while I listened to the stories of World War II veteran Lothar Marx, who'd served in the Army Signal Corps as a "skilled pigeoneer," a military instructor in the training and use of homing pigeons. The birds earned hero status during both world wars when they were used to fly secret messages through enemy lines. Marx came home to Louisville after the war, but continued to race pigeons, often competing in 500- to 600-mile, one-day races.

Of all that he'd learned about homing pigeons, he told me, how they found their way home remained a mystery.

Scientists are still pondering that puzzle. Some believe the birds have a hypersensitivity to the Earth's magnetic fields, while others suggest that sound waves, the sun and other natural factors must be involved. Whatever its guiding force, the navigational gift of homing pigeons often borders on the miraculous.

David Stephenson, a professor of journalism at the University of Kentucky who photographs and races homing pigeons as a hobby, says although most birds return home safely, he has had birds return with severe wounds from hawk attacks and buckshot pellets.

Ron Leckey of Sidney, Ohio, who has relatives in central Kentucky and has often released his racing pigeons here, visited a friend and fellow pigeon racer in northern California a few years ago. The friend shared a remarkable story about a pigeon that arrived home several days late, as wildfires were sweeping much of the region.

While driving home from work one afternoon, the friend noticed a dark-colored bird walking along the road in the direction of his house. To his amazement, it was his missing pigeon, its feathers darkened by smoke and singed by the heat encountered somewhere on its flight.

Such stories are rarely questioned by longtime pigeon racers such as Gary Potts of Frankfort and Alan Payne of Owensboro. Potts, a member of the Lexington Racing Pigeon Club, recalls one of his pigeons hobbling back into his loft on two broken legs after an unknown accident on its long flight. And Payne remembers one of his birds returning home five years after it was sold to someone 100 miles away.

Then there is the story of the pigeon that John James of Winchester shipped by air to a pigeon breeder in New Mexico. Two years later, the bird reappeared at James' loft in Winchester, having flown a distance of some 1,200 air miles to its original Kentucky home, where—after this trip—it was allowed to retire.

SEPTEMBER 2020

Chasing waterfalls

"As long as I live, I'll hear waterfalls and birds and winds sing." –John Muir

When he was 7 years old, Norman Reynolds' family visited Cumberland Falls, and Norman has loved waterfalls ever since.

By his late teens, he was hiking to every waterfall he could find. And now, five decades, a wife and two grown sons later, he has visited and photographed or collected data on approximately 350 waterfalls in some 80 of Kentucky's 120 counties.

His photographs include some falls with musical waters that spill no more than 2 or 3 feet into shaded pools, while others, such as Torrent Falls in Powell County or Yahoo Falls in McCreary County, may tumble 100 feet or more into scenic mountain streams or rock shelters once inhabited by ancient cultures. He has watched ravens soaring above their only known nesting site in Kentucky, while photographing Bad Branch Falls in Letcher County.

"There's just something, I guess for lack of a better word, 'magical' about a waterfall," Norman says. "Regardless of the size of the waterfall … depending on the surroundings, sometimes it's like another world for me."

His searches began in earnest during the mid-1980s when he noticed a postcard in a gift shop featuring picturesque Flat Lick Falls at Gray Hawk in Jackson County. He decided it would be interesting to find and photograph as many of Kentucky's waterfalls as possible. His friend Chris Anderson, who was with the Kentucky State Police, joined him in the project in the early days, but later was assigned to western Kentucky, leaving Norman to search on his own.

Their plan had been to compile a kind of field guide to Kentucky waterfalls. But eventually Norman, who lives in southern Jefferson County and works for a trucking company, got busy with his job and put the field guide on the back burner.

Because of the state's topography, most of its more impressive waterfalls are found in eastern and southeastern Kentucky, though Crowe Hollow Falls and what Norman calls "The Cliffs Cascade," both in Todd County, are notable exceptions.

Searches of topographic maps, hikes along winding streams and tips from friends and landowners help guide him to many waterfalls. He discovered an online database, www.kywaterfalls.com, which lists many falls across Kentucky, and which accepts submissions from waterfall enthusiasts.

Many of the falls are on private lands, which sometimes complicates the searches, especially when the owners cannot be reached. But Norman says he's had no problems getting permission to photograph waterfalls on most private sites.

His collection of hundreds of photos now fills many binders and digital files, arranged by county, including information about the falls' names, locations and characteristics.

Better yet, most are still flowing from his river of memories—all the way back to age 7.

OCTOBER 2020
The old oak

Just for the record, the late Willmer Pullium was not one to make up stories. "He was a straight shooter," his son-in-law, Roe Early, puts it.

I say that to begin this story—which even Willmer acknowledged no one would believe—about the old white oak tree on what then was his 100-acre farm near the Shelby-Franklin county line.

He was 75 in the fall of 1987 when he showed me the tree on the edge of a dense woodland. A scar was still visible all the way around its trunk a couple of feet off the ground. And that's where the story gets interesting.

Willmer said he had decided to cut the tree for firewood in 1963, and had made a deep cut all the way around it with a 20-inch David Bradley chain saw, until the tree began to sway back and forth as if it was about to fall. At one point, he said, it even pinched his chain saw bar until the saw stuck, then fell out when the tree rocked the other direction, leaving a gap he could have stuck his hand in.

Uncertain which direction it might fall, he backed away and waited, but it was still rocking back and forth when darkness came. So he went home, knowing it would fall that night, But early the next morning, when he went back to begin sawing it up for firewood, to his amazement the oak was still standing, but rocking dangerously back and forth as though ready to fall at any moment.

Convinced it would come crashing down in the first strong wind, Willmer gave it a wide berth ... and waited ... and waited.

But the white oak stood all winter, and when spring came, to quote Willmer, "that durn thing leafed out as pretty." The scar from his chain saw was still visible, resembling a large welding bead, but incredibly, it seemed to be healing! Then and there Willmer, a farmer, carpenter and longtime member of Shelby Energy Cooperative, declared that the old oak would never be cut down as long as he lived.

In the years that followed he often went to see it, retell the story of its survival and marvel that it was still standing. And when he died in the summer of 2003 at the age of 91, his daughter, Mary Ann Early, remembers that the minister who officiated at his funeral likened Willmer's life to that of the old oak that refused to fall.

I went back to the oak not long ago and found it still standing and in full foliage on the edge of the woodland that now has passed into the hands of Willmer's son and grandson, Gilbert Pullium Sr. and Jr.

If you know where to look, there is still a faint trace of the cut left by Willmer's chain saw 57 years ago. It now measures nearly 4 feet in diameter near the overgrown scar.

Willmer would be pleased.

JUNE 2021

Secretive sightings

A friend showed me a puzzling night photo of an animal caught on one of his trail cameras near Salt River in central Kentucky a few months ago.

I half-jokingly said it looked a little like a badger.

Such a sighting might be rare, but not impossible. Scattered reports of badgers in Kentucky have been occurring since the late 1970s when a badger was caught in a trap a few miles from the Ohio River in Breckinridge County. Then, in the spring of 1979, hunting dogs came upon two badgers and treed one of them near the Ohio River east of Belleview in Boone County. Conservation officers confirmed the sightings in each instance.

About that same time, a badger was killed on the road near Reidland in McCracken County, a few miles east of Paducah. And a few months later, another was struck by a car in Bullitt County near the Bernheim Arboretum and Research Forest exit on Interstate 65. Again, both were confirmed by conservation officers. Within a few weeks, a Kentucky state trooper saw a badger crossing I-65 in the same area.

Badgers are apparently still here, says biologist Zach Couch of the Kentucky Department of Fish and Wildlife Resources, but there is no evidence of a sizeable population beyond an occasional sighting or road kill. Nearly all the reports have been in counties bordering Indiana, where badgers were known to be extending their range. Most recent sightings in Kentucky have been in the vicinity of Owensboro.

The badger isn't the only elusive animal whose path you might one day cross in Kentucky. While larger game animals, snakes and bats get most of the public attention, several species remain virtually out of sight. Flying squirrels are believed to inhabit most counties in Kentucky, but many of us may never see one since they are most active at night. With the help of bat-like webbing between their front and back legs they may glide 100 feet or more among the trees. Their dens are usually in hollow trees, but they have been known to nest in attics.

The armadillo, which has long been associated with the Southwestern states, has established a population in Kentucky and is now fairly common in western Kentucky and several southern border counties. Couch, a consumer-member of Blue Grass Energy, says armadillo roadkills have actually been confirmed as far north as Anderson and Jessamine counties.

Finally, porcupines appear to be finding their way into the state, although not in great numbers so far. While Couch says there have probably been fewer than five credible sightings in Kentucky, he has seen reports that West Virginia has a growing porcupine population that seems to be getting well-established.

And from the feathered kingdom, the common raven is now nesting in a few locations among the cliffs in southeastern Kentucky, primarily on Pine Mountain.

The increased use of trail cameras is providing Couch and other biologists with more sightings of several secretive wildlife species.

JULY 2021

Seeds of the past, sown for the future

A scenic valley that cradles Roundstone Creek in Hart County northeast of Mammoth Cave National Park seems the perfect setting for a native seed center that is helping restore native grasses and other foundation plant life of centuries past to thousands of acres across the country.

From little bluestem, big bluestem, switch grass, spiked blazing star and dozens of other species that blanketed the prairies and tall grass savannas of pre-settlement Kentucky, Roundstone Native Seed's catalog offers more than 250 varieties of prairie and woodland plants and wildflowers.

Roundstone founders Randy Seymour and his son, John, both longtime consumer-members of Farmers Rural Electric Cooperative, never imagined today's success in 1995 when, armed only with two 5-gallon buckets, they began hand-stripping seeds from a natural stand of Indian grass in one of their fields to assist The Nature Conservancy with restoration of prairie remnants.

"It just, by word of mouth, took off," recalls Randy, 78, who credits John, 48, with guiding the business's remarkable success. But John insists it didn't happen overnight.

"From the time we first picked, it was three years before we ever sold the first seed. It just takes a long time to get seed from the wild to make it commercially available," he says.

Today, Roundstone is among the leading suppliers of native seeds in the eastern United States. It has a fleet of 17 combines or other harvesting machines, large seed cleaning and storage facilities, 32 full-time employees at its 2,000-acre farm in Hart County and other farms on contract that grow and harvest seeds in seven other states.

Among its many clients are East Kentucky Power Cooperative, which has supported Roundstone since its beginning, as well as national parks, highway projects, solar power installations, commercial landscapers, mine reclamation sites and a growing number of backyard habitat and monarch butterfly projects.

John is hopeful of adding other foundation plant varieties, including Cherokee white eagle corn, a surviving remnant of corn carried westward by members of the Cherokee Nation in its tragic, late-1830s government forced relocation known as The Trail of Tears.

Randy Seymour, who has authored a number of long-term botanical studies, partnered with his friend and mentor, botanist Julian Campbell of Lexington, several years ago on a survey of plant life in Mammoth Cave National Park, and wrote the book *Wildflowers of Mammoth Cave National Park* (University Press of Kentucky).

His lifelong interest in native plants traces to early childhood walks with his mother, Myrtle Barbour Seymour, who instilled in him a fascination with the plants and wildflowers she stopped to show him in the meadows and woodlands around their Hart County farm. Now, the family's passion for native plants continues.

"It's become a labor of love," says John, whose children work with Roundstone.

"I never got to see a prairie in Kentucky," Randy tells me, "but John is in fact bringing some of that back with what we're doing. And that truly is the highlight of my life right now."

MAY 2022

A natural

Aneighbor found a small, nonvenomous brown snake in his garden and gave it to John MacGregor when John was about 5 years old.

MacGregor smiles, reflecting on how the unusual gift helped spark his lifelong career studying snakes and a host of salamanders, frogs, bats, shrews and other non-game species.

"When I was a little kid I got interested in night crawlers, and had all these cans of night crawlers in the garage. I had a red wagon and would pour a little bit of water in the wagon and get it nice and damp, then I'd put some night crawlers in the wagon and let one can race against the other."

MacGregor is today the Kentucky state herpetologist and a legend among many of his peers. Sunni Carr-Leach, former manager of the state's Wildlife Diversity Program and currently executive director of Kentucky Nature Preserves, has said, "He is undoubtedly one of the best naturalists to ever practice here in the state."

A native of suburban Columbus, Ohio, and graduate of Ohio State University, MacGregor became a fan of University of Kentucky sports as a teenager while listening to the memorable play-by-play of his all-time favorite sports broadcaster, the late Cawood Ledford, on WHAS Radio. He later earned a master's degree at UK, and he and his wife, Lois, settled in Jessamine County.

"I decided a long time ago that where I wanted to live was pretty limited. I wanted to live somewhere that had a good diversity of salamanders," he says.

He joined the Kentucky Department of Fish and Wildlife Resources in 1981 and has traipsed across parts of every county in Kentucky, exploring caves, streams, swamps, meadows and mountains while gathering information on rare and endangered species and the distribution of everything from the cottonmouth water moccasin (easternmost distribution: the swamps along Mud River near the Butler-Muhlenberg county line), to the plains leopard frog, which he found in Fulton County in 2011; and the plateau salamander on Pine Mountain and Black Mountain in southeastern Kentucky. Yes, he's been bitten by a copperhead.

Beyond his extensive field work, MacGregor handles an average of about 600 public inquiries each year about reptiles, amphibians, vermin, various insects and unusual fungi or plants. He laments that Kentucky has no museum of natural history and that several of its major collections have been lost to museums in other states.

He served as the U.S. Forest Service endangered species specialist in the Daniel Boone National Forest for 10 years during the 1990s, but returned to Fish and Wildlife where he is still working at age 77. Currently, he is co-authoring a field guide to the state's reptiles and amphibians with University of Kentucky professor Steven Price, and Eastern Kentucky University professor Stephen Richter.

Many evenings after going home, he ventures out again in search of salamanders among the rock outcroppings in Jessamine County.

He and Lois have two daughters and four grandsons, one of whom plans to be—you guessed it—a herpetologist.

APRIL 2023

Aprils past

Sometimes, on a day in early April, when a soft breeze stirs among the spring beauties and red-winged blackbirds call from the fencerows, it's as though time rewinds for a moment to my boyhood.

When spring peepers were in full throttle and little streams rippled awake from winter sleep, I was drawn to the woods and fields.

Native river cane was plentiful then along many creeks and branches where I grew up, and I could spend hours looking for game trails in the canebrakes and tracks in the soft mud along stream banks. A hollow sycamore along a wooded stream had a doorway just large enough for me to squeeze into, and farther downstream, a crevice in a big rock above a wet-weather spring was home to spotted salamanders. I knew where wild mallards nested and where red foxes had dens.

Stories I'd read over the winter in outdoor magazines and boys' adventure books—with names like Forest Patrol and Wildlife Cameraman—had my imagination working overtime by spring. They were tales about guys who spent their lives in the woods and marshes, who drove old Jeeps and lived in cabins well off the beaten path. It sounded good to a boy of 12, but wouldn't have worked so well later with a wife and four kids. So I eventually wound up babysitting a bunch of words and stringing them together in little stories that often flow from such life memories as those of Aprils past.

Among the highlights of many Aprils as I've grown older has been the annual white bass run, during which white bass make their spring spawning migration from several of Kentucky's lakes into river tributaries.

My longtime best friend, Ron Bland of Shelby County, and I always began looking forward to the white bass run long before winter was over. Ron would oil up his fishing reels and string them with new line in January, and I'd try to find a reel that worked.

We marked calendar dates when the run began each year and kept a close eye on the redbud trees, which usually bloom about when the white bass start their migration and the water temperature reaches 55 degrees.

Ron passed away in November 2021, and I haven't had much interest in fishing since his leaving. It's just not as much fun without him around.

We often went separate ways on the river and rarely kept any fish, but we always swapped stories when the day was over—sometimes about seeing an eagle or an osprey, beaver cuttings, snakes or river otters. I once saw a chipmunk swim by when I was standing nearly hip-deep in the river. It swam from the far bank, maybe 20 yards, and several more right past me, before scampering out on the other side. I don't know if Ron believed the story, but it's true.

I wonder if that chipmunk will swim the river again this spring, when the redbuds bloom.

Electric stories, page 174

V

History

AUGUST 2013

The engine that could

For more than four decades, Carl Cruger, 85, and Joe Bratcher, 74, have carried on a steamy labor of love with a 105-ton heirloom locomotive that once was among the most celebrated on the Louisville & Nashville Railroad.

In its heyday—from 1905 until World War II—engine No. 152 pulled the L&N's premier passenger train, the Pan-American, on runs between Cincinnati and New Orleans, via Louisville. L&N advertisements proclaimed it the "master train of the South."

The numbers 1-5-2, cast in brass on the old engine's number plate, are also etched in railroad history. Teddy Roosevelt boarded No. 152 for his whistle-stop presidential campaign through Kentucky in 1912, and it carried mobster Al Capone part of the way to Alcatraz in August 1934.

Yep, 152 was on the fast track back then, both figuratively and literally. In fact, a former conductor vowed that he once clocked its speed at 105 miles per hour on a straight stretch near Horse Cave.

When it was retired in 1956 after 50 years of service, L&N's president ordered that No. 152 be spared the scrap yard and sent to the Kentucky Railway Museum, then in Louisville.

Cruger, who worked as a machinist at Louisville's Naval Ordnance plant, and Bratcher, a telephone installer, became museum volunteers in 1971. Both soon realized they had missed their calling. They should have been railroaders.

Over the next 13 years, they and other volunteers, assisted by retired L&N boilermakers, restored the engine to operating condition. It would become the first steam locomotive in the United States to be listed on the National Register of Historic Places, and it is the official state locomotive of Kentucky.

When the Kentucky Railway Museum moved to New Haven in Nelson County in 1990, Cruger, of Louisville, and Bratcher, Shepherdsville, continued to serve as master mechanics of steam operations on the volunteer crew, and often operated the engine.

Now, a new generation of volunteers has fallen in love with the old steam locomotive. Mark Johnson, 67, of New Haven thought soloing for his pilot's license was special, but it could not compare with opening the throttle on No. 152.

It was, says his fellow volunteer, locomotive engineer Tish Knoeller of Middletown, "like driving a thunderstorm."

Until recently, No. 152, the centerpiece of the Kentucky Railway Museum collection, has educated and entertained thousands of schoolchildren and rail enthusiasts of all ages on its regular 20-mile round-trip summer excursions.

Sadly, barring a financial miracle, No. 152 may have made its last run.

Since 2011, it has been parked at the museum, in need of required boiler inspection and repairs that could cost several hundred thousand dollars that the railway museum cannot afford. Cruger, Bratcher and others who love the engine and labored so long to see it run are no longer able to handle the repairs as they once did.

"It just takes a chunk out of your life," says Bratcher. "I hope that someday it'll run again."

MAY 2014

Drawing the line

Y ou may want to keep a Kentucky map handy for this one, folks.
Let your fingers do the walking along the Kentucky border to the
southwest. Be careful of the little step-up just before Lake Barkley, and then
the sudden drop-off on the west bank of Kentucky Lake. Your fingers might
start wondering if they are in Kentucky or Tennessee.

Dr. Thomas Walker must have pondered the same thing in 1779 when he
was trying to create the state line. The border established by his survey party
has been a matter of dispute between the two states for generations.

A chapter heading in James W. Sames' surveyor compilation, *Four Steps West*,
states flatly: "Mislocated Border Cost Kentucky 2,500 Sq. Miles ..."

Indeed, many professional surveyors believe that if Kentucky's southern
boundary were where it should be—it would cross Kentucky Lake about 16
miles south of where it does today. Other estimates vary from 12 to 18 miles.

That would drop Kentucky's entire southern boundary down to a straight
line even with the correctly surveyed offset of Calloway, Graves, Hickman,
and Fulton counties, placing Clarksville and many other Tennessee towns and
historic sites in Kentucky.

Surveyor Jim Adams of Bowling Green notes that in 1859, following a few

Byron Crawford takes the podium during an episode of In Performance at the Governor's Mansion, *which he hosted for KET during the 1990s.*

Melissa Warp has illustrated Crawford's columns in Kentucky Living *since he began writing for the magazine. The above is from June 2011.*

Back row, second from right, performing a railroad skit with the Cub Scout troop in Stanford.

With his pony, Dolly, and cousin Janice Garrison in the saddle.

Smiling for the camera on August 31, 1952, age 7, in Bowling Green.

With his snowman on the family farm.

Pulling the red wagon he got for Christmas, 19 1/2 months old in 1947.

Crawford's childhood home, a farmhouse in Lincoln County.

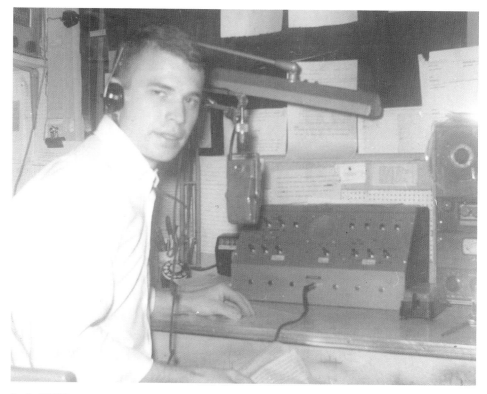

In the WAKY newsroom, mid–1960s.

Taking a call in the WHAS newsroom, early 1970s.

Running back for the Stanford High School Wildcats, 1963-64

Competing in the celebrity class of the Rock Creek Horse Show in the late 1970s.

Aboard a Charolais steer at the Harold Miller farm near Bloomfield in Nelson County.

With wife, Jackie, and their children in late 1970s.

Byron and Jackie's children: Joe, left, Wes, Eric and Andrea.

Jackie Crawford in 2022.

Eric, left, Wes, Andrea and Joe—all grown up in 1993.

Byron's father, Delbert Crawford

Byron's mother, Lucille Crawford

With Kentucky Gov. Paul Patton backstage before an episode of In Performance at the Governor's Mansion, *which Crawford hosted for KET.*

With movie director Cameron Crowe in Versailles on the set of Crowe's 2005 film, Elizabethtown.

other attempts at correcting the line, both states gave up on yet another survey after discovering exactly how far south a corrected Kentucky line would have to be moved, how many Tennesseans would become overnight Kentuckians, and what a bureaucratic boondoggle would ensue. Heavy stone markers were set, essentially along the old "Walker line," denoting the official boundary.

Hearsay has it that a landowner below the mysterious notch in Simpson County offered surveyors a barrel of whiskey to leave his place in Tennessee.

"Tennessee has been fortunate in nearly all of her disputes as to state boundaries," former Tennessee Supreme Court Associate Justice Samuel Cole Williams wrote in a 1930 publication. "Her chief gains, in the match of wits, have been at the expense of Virginia and Kentucky."

Paris, Tennessee, surveyor Larry I. Smith agrees with that. "We did all right," he says with a smile.

In time, what once was a point of serious contention between the two states has been reduced to good-natured joking.

In fact, in 1990 surveyors from the two states joined in a search for the 64 stone markers that, in the 1850s, were set along the border from Bell County in the east to Fulton in the west.

"We found 38 of them," says Adams, recalling that one had been used for some years as a weight on a local farmer's disk harrow, until he found out how important it was and returned it to its place in the middle of a field.

Another of the displaced boundary markers—with "KY.–TENN." chiseled on the sides—is on exhibit at the South Central Kentucky Cultural Center on Water Street in Glasgow.

MAY 2015

Still standing

When he was a boy of about 12, James H. Riley and some of his buddies—armed with little more than axes, handsaws and their boyhood imaginations—built themselves a crude log cabin in a woodland on the back of the Marshall County farm where Riley grew up.

He remembered the venture while recounting how, in the 1980s and '90s, he collected an entire village of original log buildings, one building at a time, from scattered sites around Kentucky and west Tennessee, and relocated them to his farm near Benton.

It all began when a neighbor gave Riley an old log corncrib if he would move it. Then he found a log barn in Spencer County, which he hauled to western Kentucky and attached to the corn crib.

That was all he had planned to do, until his brother-in-law mentioned a friend in Lyon County who had a circa-1840s "story and a half" log cabin that he'd give to Riley. The small log village, clustered on a hillside on Riley's farm, eventually grew to 13 buildings.

He called it Cabin Hill.

Soon, he added a smokehouse and another corncrib—this one with double dovetail notches—part of another cabin from near Nicholasville, and the largest building, a 35-by-25-foot schoolhouse from Dover, Tennessee, made of yellow poplar logs and said to have been built by Civil War veterans.

As Riley numbered and carefully reassembled each log in its place, the more he came to admire those whose hands had originally cut, hewed, notched and fitted each log together, perhaps a century and a half earlier.

It was possible, he reasoned, that many who had shaped these logs could not read and write, but they certainly could build structures that stood the test of time.

Today, most of the buildings are furnished with relics of the pioneer period. The log school now houses what Riley calls The Spit 'n' Whittle General Store, with a long counter, a big potbellied stove, a flour barrel from a vanished general store and other artifacts.

Cabin Hill enjoyed several years of visits from school groups, historical societies and the media, but now is a virtual ghost town of gray log monuments to a way of life that is all but forgotten. Riley donated one of the cabins to a group of high school students from Wylie, Texas, who reassembled the structure in Wylie, but the other buildings are still there. And Riley, a member of West Kentucky RECC, still has a few old-fashioned surprises, and occasionally a new one, for passersby at Cabin Hill.

Each winter he taps many of his sugar maple trees to make maple syrup. One cold day his friend Sam Clark noticed that Riley had attached a tap and sap bucket to a utility pole—and he stopped to ask what that was for.

Riley, who had been hoping someone would ask, smiled and answered: "Pole syrup."

JUNE 2015

Monumental thanks

The mountains of eastern Kentucky cradle many fascinating stories that have been passed down, mostly by word of mouth, through generations of families who've inhabited once-remote, small communities in the region.

So it is with a stone sculpture hidden deep in a tangle of vines and timber a few hundred yards up a steep hillside in southern Owsley County, on the right fork of Island Creek, just over 8 miles south of Booneville.

As the story goes, the sculpture dates to the Great Depression years of the early 1930s, when an itinerant "pack peddler"—selling items, house-to-house, from a pack on his back—fell ill while passing through Owsley County and was befriended by the John Williams Sr. family, who lived near the base of the surrounding hills.

The late Joyce Wilson, an Owsley County historian, would write 40 years later that the peddler was 70-year-old Granville Johnson, of whom little is known, except that he had claimed to be a stone carver.

The nature of his illness is not recorded, but he spent most of that summer with the Williams family while recuperating.

As he recovered, he often disappeared with hammer and chisel into the shadows of the hills, and was sometimes gone for hours.

When finally he was ready to move on, Johnson led the family up a hillside to a sandstone outcropping where he had carved for them a life-sized, bas-relief likeness of Abraham Lincoln in a large sandstone boulder, as a gift of his appreciation for the great kindness they had shown him.

The sculpture is close to Lincoln's actual height, about 6 feet, 4 inches, and bears a striking likeness, said Owsley County Judge-Executive Cale Turner. Lincoln is holding a Bible in his left hand, but for reasons unknown the right hand and lower forearm were not finished.

Perhaps due in part to its obscure location, the sculpture, which is now included on a Smithsonian Art Museum list of Kentucky outdoor sculptures, was virtually forgotten until it was brought to public attention several years ago. Owsley County Fiscal Court has since acquired the sculpture and surrounding acreage and hopes to open a trail leading to the site.

Wilson's story of the sculpture, which is part of the Owsley County Historical Society's collection, notes that the boulder in which the sculpture is carved had been part of a larger sandstone formation until it gave way and tumbled some distance down the hillside, coming to rest on an edge that presented a natural surface suitable for the carving.

She wrote that Granville Johnson was never heard from again after he left the Williams place that summer.

Molly Turner, executive director of the Owsley County Action Team and member of Jackson Energy Cooperative, says the statue stands as a monument to the goodness of an Owsley County family, and to the pride of a man who wanted to repay that kindness in the only way he knew how.

AUGUST 2015

Piecing memories

A patchwork of homespun memories has followed Bobbie Smith Bryant from the family farm of her 1960s childhood in rural Calloway County—all the way across Kentucky.

She and her brother, Billy Dale Smith, had the good fortune while growing up of learning not only from their parents, but from both sets of grandparents and great-grandparents. Some of their stories seem as fresh to Bobbie today as when she first heard them as a little girl.

One of her grandfathers owned a country store at Kirksey in northwestern Calloway County, where she and Billy Dale listened wide-eyed to older folks trade tales of the past, debate events of the day, and compare their crops of dark-fired tobacco. At bedtime on cold nights, they were often tucked under one of their grandmothers' hand-stitched quilts.

When quilts were hung on the clothesline to air out on a nice day, Bobbie was fascinated by the colorful patterns with odd names: Flower Garden, Wedding Ring, Lone Star, Drunkard's Path, Jacob's Ladder, and others.

It may never have occurred to her then that long after she had moved away from the family farm, studied business at Murray State University, and become a community development advisor with the Kentucky League of Cities, living near Louisville, she would reach back for those memories to share with other generations of Kentuckians.

A few years ago, as she began to appreciate more fully her family genealogy and to realize that the way of life she had known in the Jackson Purchase Region was rapidly changing, she began writing about western Kentucky's cultural and social traditions, and telling others about them across the state as a presenter with the Kentucky Humanities Council.

Her first book, *Forty Acres and a Red Belly Ford: The Smith Family of Calloway County,* revisits life on the Smith family farm. She later helped produce *Farming in the Black Patch*, a public television documentary about dark tobacco farming in western Kentucky.

"The catalyst that nudged me toward books, filmmaking and speaking across the state came when I discovered how little had previously been written, or was known, about western Kentucky," she says.

Her second book, *Passions of the Black Patch: Cooking and Quilting in Western Kentucky,* features more than 200 regional recipes, more stories and a collection of quilts. Together, she and her brother have 23 quilts that have been passed down through their family. And wrapped in some of those quilts are stories as colorful as the quilt pieces.

"I remember Mother talking about when she was a little girl, not much more than a toddler, her parents were hoeing tobacco and her mother had put her out on a quilt pallet (that's what they called them when they used them outside on the ground), and a big snake crawled up next to her on the pallet. Their dog, Buster, attacked the snake and kept it from harming my mother."

MAY 2016

A bit of where we came from

Lovers of Kentucky's covered bridges will be pleased to learn that the state's longest timbered span still in existence—the Beech Fork Bridge in northwestern Washington County—is being restored.

Work begins this spring on the picturesque 210-foot-long structure, often called the Mooresville or Mount Zion Bridge, which was built soon after the Civil War and carried traffic on State Route 458 until it was bypassed in 1977.

Beech Fork is one of only 13 authentic covered bridges remaining in Kentucky where once there were well over 700. Washington County alone had at least 18 covered bridges within its boundaries, and shared five others with neighboring counties Anderson and Nelson, according to Walter Laughlin, co-author of *Kentucky's Covered Bridges*.

If the old bridge could talk, it certainly would include a story remembered by Roger Hahn of Mt. Washington, about his brother, David, and two friends from Louisville who were driving out to meet some girls from nearby Willisburg many years ago.

The driver from the city was evidently unfamiliar with covered bridges and mistook the bridge for a barn in the middle of the road. When he suddenly swerved left to avoid the "building," the car went tumbling down an embankment, coming to rest on its side against a small tree beside the Beech Fork River. All three boys escaped serious injury, if not humiliation.

Despite much confusion over the years as to who built the Beech Fork Bridge, Dale Salmon of the Mt. Washington Historical Society says his search of old records in Washington County indicates that the two-span burr arch truss was built by brothers Henry J. and William P. Barnes of Mt. Washington, and that the bridge was completed in 1871.

Now listed on the National Register of Historic Places, the bridge has long been a popular subject for artists and photographers, and a favorite local landmark. During the early 1980s, after flooding damaged the bridge's pier, the late Richard Hamilton, a retired Washington County highway contractor, donated his time and equipment to make repairs, using sandstone that had been quarried in 1895.

Current repairs are being done by Arnold M. Graton of New Hampshire, whom *Yankee* magazine called "the man who saves covered bridges."

"Most of the timbers that we'll be working with are original to the bridge, primarily poplar and oak, and we can probably re-use or leave in place 70% of it," Graton says.

Kentucky Heritage Council architect Jen Spangler Williamson notes that, wherever possible, the bridge's original fabric and historic integrity will be preserved.

Since 2004, when Graton first came to Kentucky to help with restoration work on the Goddard Covered Bridge in Fleming County, he has returned to Kentucky to work on the Cabin Creek Bridge in Lewis County and the Johnson Creek Bridge in Robertson County.

"I think it's important to save them for the same reason it's important to save the memory of your folks," says Graton. "We need a little bit of where we came from."

Editor's note: The Beech Fork Bridge was destroyed by fire in March 2021.

FEBRUARY 2016

To love the pure and good

After sleeping most of a century in obscurity, the poetry of Effie Waller Smith has reawakened to new life through a twist of fate befitting one of her lyric works.

Effie Waller was born in the rural Chloe Creek community of Pike County in 1879 to former enslaved couple Frank and Sibbie Ratliff Waller. The African American Registry notes that she was raised in a farm home "in which God was heavily praised and education highly prized."

So began the life of a woman who stood only 5 feet tall, but whose image in the mirror of time grows ever larger in reflection of her poetic legacy to African American literature in Appalachia.

Inspired by the beauty of the mountains and streams she explored as a child, she was setting her thoughts to poetry by age 16:

"…How oft their grandeur I've admired/ As 'neath them I have stood;/ And it was they that me inspired/ To love the pure and good."

Trained as a teacher at what is now Kentucky State University in Frankfort between 1900 and 1902, she taught school for several years in Kentucky and Tennessee, as her poetry flowered into longer forms and short stories. The simultaneous triumph and terminus of her publishing career came in 1917 when her sonnet *Autumn Winds* appeared in the prestigious *Harper's Monthly* magazine of culture and the arts. It was to be her last known published work.

She would soon join a religious commune in Waukesah, Wisconsin, eventually moving to Neenah, Wisconsin, where she died in 1960. She had lost an infant child, and her husband, a sheriff's deputy, had been murdered in Pike County in the line of duty. She had published three books of poetry that were all but forgotten by the time she died.

Then one day in the late 1960s, Pikeville College librarian Bruce Brown handed W. David Deskins, a junior English major and writer of poetry, an old book of Effie Waller Smith's poems that had been found in an attic, and said, "Tell me what you think about this."

Deskins' eyes fixed upon a poem titled *Memories of Home*:

"Down below the apple orchard/ From a fern-clad mossy bank/ Where the naiads love to linger,/ Where the elders tall and rank,

And the willows cast their shadows,/ Where the night birds sweetly sing/ To the moonlight and the starlight,/ Bubbled forth a sylvan spring..."

Moved by her work, Deskins copied the poem, but laid it aside and did not rediscover it until 15 years later. He then embarked upon a determined, one-man quest to bring Effie Waller Smith's poetry and life story to public recognition.

Now a retired Pike County circuit court clerk, Deskins has written the introduction to *The Collected Works of Effie Waller Smith* for the Schomburg Library's *Nineteenth-Century Black Women Writers* series (Oxford University Press), and is currently writing her literary biography.

Recently told that, due primarily to his efforts, Effie Waller Smith's poetry is now being taught in many African American literary courses across the nation, Deskins recalls, "I think I cried."

MARCH 2017

Long live old wood

Picture a wall in your home or business framed with a rustic stall door from one of the broodmare barns at Lexington's storied Faraway Farm—the one-time home of Man o' War and War Admiral.

Longwood Antique Woods of Lexington is reclaiming history most elegantly.

Old timber frame barns that have outlived their usefulness on the farm, long-abandoned tobacco warehouses, tumbled down log buildings and other structures that might otherwise face destruction are instead finding new life in today's finest interiors through the woodshop at Longwood.

George Gatewood, Longwood's 46-year-old president, is a lifelong friend of old barn wood.

As a boy of 8 on his family's Montgomery County estate—also named Longwood—he used boards from an old barn on the place to build a treehouse connecting two of the large trees whose foliage formed a canopy above the long avenue leading to the antebellum residence.

George would later study graphic arts, and even work for a few years reclaiming strip-mine sites in eastern Kentucky, before coming back to old barn wood.

After a tornado destroyed several barns in Montgomery County, George and

160

his father, David, salvaged some of the barn wood and sold it to a company in Boston that was milling the lumber for use in New England's upscale interiors.

Soon, the Gatewoods began milling old lumber themselves, repurposing timbers of Kentucky's vanishing landscape for eventual re-use in more exclusive settings.

Although their projects have taken them from West Palm Beach to Laguna Beach to Long Island, the majority of their clients are in central Kentucky, where the history of their woods is most appreciated.

Many of Kentucky's major bourbon distillers have found Longwood's repurposed woods lend the perfect blend of warmth and nostalgia to their visitor centers. And *Garden & Gun* magazine used wood from a barn that was removed from Churchill Downs a few years ago for its office interiors in Charleston, South Carolina.

Reclaimed oak boards from the many miles of plank fence that crisscross legendary Bluegrass horse farms are being milled for Longwood's Thoroughbred Oak flooring collection.

Longwood purchases some of the old buildings and fences for recycling, but owners of many doomed structures often just want them to be removed and saved.

The boards from horse barns sometimes have uneven edges from having been nibbled on (or "cribbed") by unknown thoroughbreds with a habit for chewing on wood.

In 2004, Longwood began dismantling 13 barns at Hamburg Place on the outskirts of Lexington, which in the early 20th century produced five Kentucky Derby winners, including 1919 Triple Crown winner Sir Barton. Alysheba, the 1987 Derby and Preakness winner, was also bred at Hamburg.

In one of the Hamburg barns, history had hidden a surprise for George. He discovered, in an old trunk, a letter to Hamburg's colorful founder, John E. Madden, from legendary Wild West lawman William B. "Bat" Masterson.

APRIL 2017

Preserving an ancestry

Growing up on the Kahnawake Mohawk Indian Reserve in Quebec, Canada, during the 1950s, Susan Mitchell Mullins could scarcely have imagined that the stories her grandmother shared with her during their walks through the woods beside the Saint Lawrence River would one day find their way to thousands of young Kentuckians.

Yet a few decades later, as a resident of southern Madison County and member of Blue Grass Energy Cooperative, Susan now recounts for Kentucky school students the stories, nature lore and beliefs of the Mohawk culture passed down from her grandmother along those wilderness pathways.

Born to Angus and Dorothy Deer in 1946, Susan's given Mohawk name was Kwaronhia:wi, which means "sunset over the river." Her family changed their surname to Mitchell to avoid prejudice and better fit into society beyond the reserve. Many Mohawk men took jobs as ironworkers on New York's skyscrapers, including her father and several uncles and cousins, some of whom would help build the United Nations headquarters and the World Trade Center. Because so many Mohawks worked in skyscraper construction, they earned a reputation for being unafraid of heights.

When she was 11, Susan and a number of other Mohawk children were sent to a Catholic school in nearby Brooklyn, New York, but returned to the reserve on weekends and in summer. She later studied business at Brooklyn College, and wound up working as a bookkeeper for a thoroughbred horse owner who had farms in several states, including Kentucky—which brought her to the Bluegrass.

After the horseman died and the farms changed hands, Susan opened a jewelry store.

"I was doing really well, then one day a teacher came in and said, 'Susan, you're an American Indian. Would you mind coming to our school and telling us a little bit about it?'"

Soon she was being invited to more schools to tell stories about her life on the Mohawk Reserve, where her daughter, two grandchildren and several other family members still make their home.

Now, as a member of the Kentucky Arts Council's Arts Registry, the Berea College Promise Neighborhoods program and a member of the Kentucky Native American Commission, she devotes much of her time to helping young Kentuckians glimpse her fascinating Mohawk heritage.

She explains that the Mohawks are part of the Iroquois Nation, which once encompassed much of the Kentucky territory, and reminds students that many of their families may have Native American ancestry whose history has been lost. She tells them how the Mohawks respect and care for the older generations and Mother Earth, and encourages them to develop good study habits and stay in school.

"I feel honored that somebody wants to know about my people," she says. "What makes me happy is being able to continue to work with students and hope they understand the value of getting a good education so they can live a good life as adults."

JUNE 2017

A museum for Monticello

As Robert G. Breeding was building a hotel in downtown Monticello in 1935—using mules, shovels and hand labor to dig the basement—he discovered a cave beneath the site.

Wayne County is crisscrossed with many miles of mostly unmapped and unexplored caverns, and after Breeding apparently decided the cave posed no danger to the building, he came up with a plan to put it to good use. He sank a shaft about the diameter of a manhole cover more than 20 feet down into the cave—where temperatures were in the mid-50s—and used fans to circulate the cool air through the hotel during the warm months.

Museum director and curator David Smith recalls stories of, when there was a restaurant at the hotel, fruits and vegetables being stored around the mouth of the air shaft to keep them fresh—until some locals found a way to enter the cave from the outside, climb up the shaft and help themselves to the produce. After a few years, the moist cave air became a problem in the hotel, and commercial air conditioning was installed.

In addition to its 35 guest rooms, the Hotel Breeding also provided retail space for a bank, a furniture store, a Western Auto and Ben Franklin store and meeting rooms for civic clubs.

By the 1980s, business at the hotel had declined to the point that it was converted to a rooming house. It had been vacant several years when it was purchased in 1997 by the Wayne County Historical Society.

Now, the refurbished Colonial Revival style landmark, listed on the National Register of Historic Places, is home to the Wayne County Museum and is once again a focal point of downtown Monticello. Nearly all of its rooms are filled with artifacts of the county's colorful past.

One of the first-floor exhibits is a full-sized reproduction of the Monticello-Burnside stagecoach, believed to have been the last stagecoach operating east of the Mississippi River. The original, which was stored for years in Monticello, is now on exhibit at the Wells Fargo Museum in Los Angeles.

Visitors from 30 states toured the Wayne County museum last year to view relics from prehistoric ages to the more recent past. A museum volunteer, 89-year-old Juanita Coffey, enjoys demonstrating antique folk toys from the museum's "Attic" exhibit of odd pieces.

One of the second-floor exhibits is dedicated to musicians from Wayne County, including fiddler "Blind Dick" Burnett, whose early 20th-century song *I Am a Man of Constant Sorrow* was popularized in the motion picture *O Brother, Where Art Thou?*

Fittingly, the basement where Breeding sank an air shaft to cool the hotel with cave air now has an entire room devoted to local caves. The room's centerpiece is a small enclosure, capped by acrylic glass, through which visitors can peer into the lighted shaft at the illuminated cave floor 23 feet below, and see the cavern much as Breeding may have seen it in 1935.

SEPTEMBER 2019

Western Flyer

A story that began with American novelist John Steinbeck and his best friend, marine biologist Edward Ricketts, in 1940 has found its way from the Pacific Northwest coast to the forests of Kentucky.

Steinbeck and Ricketts spent 6 1/2 weeks that year aboard a leased 1930s fishing vessel called the *Western Flyer* while on an ecology study of the Sea of Cortez between the Baja Peninsula and the Mexican mainland. Their nonfiction books about the expedition, *The Sea of Cortez*, and later *Log from the Sea of Cortez*, have slept most of their shelf lives in the shadows of Steinbeck's giant classics, *The Grapes of Wrath*, *Of Mice and Men* and other works of Pulitzer and Nobel acclaim.

But back to the *Western Flyer*.

Long after Steinbeck and Ricketts were gone, the old boat they'd immortalized was still around, though it had sunk three-and-a-half times.

In 2016, a group of scientists and others who had been influenced, if not inspired, by Ricketts' and Steinbeck's studies bought the 77-foot long boat and created a foundation to restore it as a working ecological research memorial.

This ultimately led Western Flyer Project Director Chris Chase to Kentucky from the restoration site in Port Townsend, Washington.

"There are certain materials that can only be used in certain applications, and one of those is white oak," Chase says. The frame, or rib cage, of the boat is steam-bent into shape from perfectly straight white oak beams.

For nearly three years, Chase searched forests from coast to coast for white oak of suitable quality, before his quest ended in Kentucky. With assistance from master logger Holger Groessler of Louisville and Berea College forester Clint Patterson, he was able to acquire prime logs from a 9,000-acre forest managed by the college and from a small private woodland in Anderson County.

For the critical task of sawing them into unblemished 18-foot, 3-by-4-inch beams, Chase turned to sawyer David Merchant, who operates a small custom sawmill near Bagdad in Shelby County.

"I wasn't looking for a deal," Chase insists. "I was looking for perfection. And David was phenomenal. Everybody in Kentucky was top shelf."

Merchant, a retired middle school science teacher and consumer-member of Shelby Energy Cooperative, says he "kind of felt honored" that he was trusted with sawing the white oak for the boat, but adds that he thought any good sawyer could do it if they took the time and had pride in their work.

Already the Western Flyer Project has drawn the attention of the *National Geographic* and *Smithsonian* magazines, and others are watching the boat's remarkable rebirth around a heart of Kentucky white oak.

And back in Kentucky, David Merchant now has a perfect answer for friends who are always asking, "Have you sawed anything interesting lately?"

APRIL 2020

Tell stories again

L ittle is left of the rural landscape I knew as a boy.

The meadows and woodlands that framed my world in those days now sleep beneath the glow of security lights, under modern homes, paved streets, privacy fences and manicured shrubbery.

Recalling the countryside as it was back then brings to mind the crossing of a small stream on the nearly 1-mile walk along the graveled lane between our farm and the school bus stop on the main highway. Knotty apples from a lonesome old tree nearby weren't much bigger than a golf ball, and nearly as hard and tasteless. But I usually sampled one of them every year before pitching it into the stream and watching it drift away.

Although the stream wasn't on our land, I felt some ownership in knowing that it eventually meandered to the creek that bordered our back fields. In those days, I knew the creeks and their branches, the lay of the land and practically every family within a 2-mile radius of our place.

Sometimes I wonder what the children who now live where I lived as a boy will remember about growing up in that same place. Will their memories have any ties with the land and community, or will they be mostly of digital images?

The subject came up during a visit with Martin Cothran, an educational writer and speaker, who lives near Danville.

Cothran sees the decline of the agricultural economy—and ultimately the loss of community—as the biggest cultural event of our generation; a crisis that most don't recognize.

There aren't many "real places" that approximate a community anymore, only locations, he told me. And the internet has created a kind of separate reality in which "now" is never enough—with a new "now" always waiting just over the next digital rise. The past and the future are virtually lost in the new, distracted present of a digital world that has no location at all.

We are distancing ourselves from natural things such as trees, streams and wildlife, and are surrounding ourselves with the artificial.

Highly mobile careers and technological advances mean that many families may now live farther apart and see each other less, often further disconnecting children from the stories and cultural heritage once shared by older relatives.

Cothran believes the closing of many community schools—the traditional centerpieces of most small communities—along with a disturbing de-emphasis in teaching state and local history are among other factors helping to sap our cultural energy.

While some issues are beyond our immediate control, he insists we could and should be teaching today's young people the history of their state and communities.

"We need to make schools once again a means of connecting the generations," he says. "History, at its best, is storytelling, and we don't tell stories anymore. If we tell kids these stories they will love them, but we're not doing that."

Let's hope it's not too late to start again.

MARCH 2022

Above and beyond

The story goes that when John Paul Riddle was a kid in Pike County at the dawn of the 1900s, he'd sometimes lie on his back watching birds soar in the summer sky as he dreamed of flying.

His grandmother even claimed that when he was very small he once tried to plant some feathers—hoping to grow enough birds to learn their secrets.

Paul's mother, a teacher, died when he was 2 1/2, and he and his two sisters, ages 1 and 4, were cared for by their maternal grandmother.

Young Paul was bright, adventurous and ambitious. He had a paper route, tended cattle for a neighbor on Shelby Creek, cleaned the Methodist and Presbyterian churches with a friend and took correspondence courses in auto mechanics and aviation. At the insistence of his father, a teacher and later a postmaster in Pike County, he carried a pocket dictionary nearly every place he went as a boy.

After graduation from Pikeville College Academy, he accepted an appointment to the United States Naval Academy in Annapolis, where he stayed only one year before leaving in 1920 to pursue his true love—flying. Twenty-two years after the Wright brothers' first flight, Riddle was barnstorming and stunt flying out of Lunken Airport in Cincinnati.

Biographer Kim Sheeter mused that she knew her research of Riddle's life wouldn't be boring after discovering that he would sometimes dress as a woman and pretend to be a spectator in the crowd while waiting for the air shows to begin—only to dash from among the startled onlookers and take off in a plane to perform a series of daredevil stunts. On July 4, 1923, he flew his Curtiss Jenny bi-wing under Pikeville's Middle Bridge.

In Cincinnati, he made friends with local flying enthusiast Higbee Embry, with whom he founded Embry-Riddle Flying School, and later Embry-Riddle Aviation Corporation, which contracted to fly "air-mail" between Cincinnati and Chicago. That business eventually grew into American Airlines.

After Embry left the partnership, Riddle and another partner, John McKay, re-formed Embry-Riddle School of Aviation in Florida. The school trained many U.S. and Royal Air Force pilots for service in World War II.

Riddle's son remembers finding among his father's papers a picture of Sir Winston Churchill, seated in the family's living room during a visit with his dad.

In the mid-1940s Riddle left the flying school to pursue other aviation ventures, but he would later serve on the board of what now is known as Embry-Riddle Aeronautical University, one of the world's foremost flight training schools. In addition to campuses in Daytona Beach, Florida, and Prescott, Arizona, it has other training facilities worldwide.

John Paul Riddle died in Florida in 1989 at the age of 87. His ashes were scattered from a plane piloted by an airline captain who graduated from Embry-Riddle Aeronautical University. It was a fitting departure for the Kentucky aviation pioneer whose boyhood dreams have helped carry several generations into skies above the birds and beyond the clouds.

SEPTEMBER 2022

Friend of history

Looking at Facebook, I was surprised to see a photo of 19th century Kentucky giant, Capt. Martin Van Buren Bates, looking back at me. Bates, of Letcher County, stood 7 feet, 9 inches by some accounts, and 7 feet, 11 inches by others.

You might say Facebook is "friending" Kentucky history through the words of Sam Terry IV, a Barren County historian and consumer-member of Farmers RECC, who daily posts brief narratives of the state's history on anniversary dates related to story subjects: The New Madrid earthquake, the death of cave explorer Floyd Collins, the last broadcast of University of Kentucky play-by-play icon Cawood Ledford, the winning jockey in the first Kentucky Derby and more than 500 others so far.

History has had a hold on Sam since he was a child—wandering among family heirlooms and listening to stories in his grandparents' rural Barren County home.

He didn't realize it at the time, but says, "there was an almost daily thread of history that ran through our lives in the telling and retelling of recollections about people, objects or just a recalled moment in time."

His grandfather had been orphaned at age 17 on the day he graduated from high school, and felt a special need to pass along to his only grandchild an appreciation of family history and regional culture.

The grandfather's legacy was enriched by high school teacher Gladys Wilson, an accomplished genealogist, who instructed Sam in research techniques and recommended him as her replacement as researcher for local records requests received by the county clerk's office. Sam started his own genealogical research service while still in high school.

After earning a degree in history and political science at Transylvania University and later serving with the state's Division of Historic Properties, he returned to the family farm in Barren County, where he still lives. Although he now holds a marketing and communications position with a multistate corporation, history keeps calling him back.

He has hosted walking tours of the Glasgow Municipal Cemetery and even a regular local cable television program devoted to "Faces and Places in the Barrens."

Occasionally, a calendar date would remind him of something noteworthy that happened in Kentucky, and one day in the summer of 2018—on the anniversary of Kentucky gaining statehood—he decided to write a paragraph about it and post it on his Facebook page. Soon he was posting such accounts daily. At the suggestion of a friend he called it, *Sam Terry's Kentucky.*

He wondered if people would really read history on a social media platform and, if so, how long it could be sustained. But the number of Facebook viewers has grown to approximately 27,000 per day—with the reach in one month eclipsing more than 1.1 million who either read or reacted to the posts.

His goal of instilling pride in Kentucky through knowledge and appreciation of its history is bringing many forgotten faces and places to Facebook.

OCTOBER 2022

Electric stories

One of my early childhood memories is watching a lineworker from Inter-County Energy climb the "light pole" that stood near our farmhouse, and being fascinated by his climbing gear. We knew him as "the REA man."

I didn't know at the time that REA stood for Rural Electrification Administration—the agency created in the mid-1930s to help provide electrical service to rural areas not served by private utilities—but I knew that "the REA man" kept the lights on at our place.

In those days most members took their own meter readings on a card provided by the cooperative, then mailed the card back to the office along with their payment for the previous month.

Many rural members had no phones at that time and Mike Cobb, president of Owen Electric Cooperative, says he's heard stories that customers would occasionally write a note on one of the cards, notifying the cooperative that their power was out. It wasn't uncommon back then for farmers to invite line crews to a meal, or to offer their work horses or mules for pulling lines or dragging poles.

Phyllis Oliver, manager of office services at Salt River Electric, recalls some years ago a Spencer County member who always maintained a credit of about

$1,000 when paying her electric bill, despite not having much money. When asked about it, the woman explained that she had a terminal illness and wanted to make sure everything was taken care of for her husband who did not read well and would struggle with handling bills when she was gone. Phyllis was able to help.

Another woman had lost her only son to cancer, then had lost his beloved dog, Rusty, which she buried near him. Later, when another member was in the office and mentioned that he could no longer care for his dog and was hoping to find a new home for the animal, Phyllis put him in touch with the woman who had lost her son's dog. She was happy to adopt the new dog, and even happier when she learned his name was Rusty.

In the summer of 1992, when I was writing for a newspaper, I visited the rural Butler County community of Quality when 83-year-old Rachel Hudnall got electricity for the first time in the home that her father-in-law had built upon his return from the Civil War. It was there I first met Eston Glover, then the communications officer with the Hopkinsville-based Pennyrile Electric. We both came to see how Mrs. Hudnall liked electricity.

"It's all right," she told us. "I turned it on yesterday and heated some water. It was red hot in a second."

Now a retired president of Pennyrile Electric, Glover counts as one of many memorable moments the day Rachel Hudnall put aside her kerosene lamps after 83 years, and turned on the electric lights.

"I might get an electric skillet or something like that," she told us as we were leaving.

All-star memories, page 186

VI

Sports

MARCH 2013

Hardwood heaven

Once upon a time—when weather-beaten basketballs rattled rickety rims on dirt courts across Kentucky—it was not unusual to hear young boys yell out the name King Kelly Coleman or that of some other high school basketball star when they made a spectacular shot.

Coleman once scored 75 points and grabbed 41 rebounds for his team, the Wayland Wasps of Floyd County, in a game against an archrival during the 1950s.

Farther west, in Muhlenberg County, the name Raymond "Corky" Withrow echoed off many backboards for miles around Central City High School, where Withrow's amazing talents became the stuff of legend, and where the original gym in which he played is now a museum.

If you grew up in Kentucky during basketball's golden age of the late 1940s, '50s and early '60s, you could fill the remaining lines of this story with memories of your own heroes—Freddie Maggard of Carr Creek; Howie Crittenden and Charles "Doodle" Floyd from Cuba, Kentucky; Mason Cope (1949 Converse National Player of the Year) of Brewers; Taylor County's Clem Haskins; Adrian Smith of Farmington; Owensboro's Cliff Hagan and Bobby Rascoe; Frank Ramsey of Madisonville; Jim McDaniels, Scottsville; Butch Beard from Breckinridge County; Wes Unseld with Louisville's Seneca High School; and on and on.

In 2006, Charles Thurman of Sonora and his longtime friend and fellow history buff Sherrill Williams of Vine Grove read Gary West's book *King Kelly Coleman—Kentucky's Greatest Basketball Legend*, and were so moved by the story and the boyhood memories it evoked that they asked West to introduce them to the reclusive Coleman.

When they learned that Coleman and his friend Jerry Fultz were trying to create a Mountain Sports Hall of Fame at the old Wayland gym where Coleman played, Thurman and Williams, with help from West, organized a fundraising dinner at Claudia's Tea Room and the Thurman-Phillips Guest Home, which Thurman and his wife, Claudia, operate in Sonora. Many of the state's notable players from yesteryear were invited.

Later, for the first time since the 1956 state high school basketball tournament, Coleman and Withrow met again, this time in Wayland, along with Freddie Maggard, who had hit the winning shot against both of their teams to lead Carr Creek to the title that year.

To make a long story much too short, Thurman and Williams, with help from West and many others across the commonwealth, have now visited and interviewed on video dozens of legendary Kentucky stars who are still around to tell their stories.

The interviews with former players continue, while in Wayland (population around 450) Coleman and Fultz are still working to create the Mountain Sports Hall of Fame and museum in hopes of preserving much of eastern Kentucky's sports history where many sports legends were born.

JULY 2014

Nostalgia in the corner pocket

My longtime friend and onetime eight-ball opponent, Ron Bland of Bagdad, asked the other day what's happened to all the poolrooms that once were fixtures in most towns across Kentucky.

"The answer is that small-town poolrooms went away with farming," according to Gunnar Graven, vice president of Louisville's Steepleton Company, which for generations has supplied tables and other equipment to poolrooms across Kentucky, Indiana and Tennessee.

Time was when many farmers had breakfast or lunch at the local pool hall, and then spent hours shooting pool, especially in the winter months and on rainy days when they couldn't work in the fields. But as weekend farmers with other careers replaced retiring full-time farmers, an estimated 70-80% of Kentucky's poolrooms vanished.

All that lingers of many of these sanctuaries of secondhand smoke are colorful recollections of characters who passed through their doors, and aromatic, onion-laced memories of hamburgers, chili dogs and other tasty foods from their grills. Some of the recipes were—and still are—closely guarded secrets.

Clyde Honaker Jr. of Lexington remembers "meal burgers" were the claim to fame of Jimmy "Hick" Warner's poolroom in his hometown of Owingsville in Bath County. Hick's wife, Margaret, mixed the hamburger with cornmeal and reportedly could get 18 to 20 burgers out of a pound of ground beef. They sold for 10 cents each with a slice of onion and mustard at no extra charge.

Kenneth Croslin of Warren County tells of seeing his brother Tommy shooting pool at Simpson's poolroom in Bowling Green when a cue ball jumped the table on a break and splashed smack-dab in the middle of a bystander's bowl of that poolroom's beloved beef stew.

Most poolrooms didn't allow women until well into the 1970s. There's a long-ago story of a gruff poolroom owner in the rural Mason County village of Mayslick who is said to have turned away several members of an out-of-town motorcycle gang and their female companions with the matter-of-fact greeting: "Sorry, fellas, we don't allow women in here."

Ed Waggener of Columbia remembers that when he was a student at Lindsey Wilson College back when there were only 142 students at the Adair County school, chapel was mandatory and one of the dean's jobs was to patrol Columbia's poolrooms to find absentees from chapel on Wednesday mornings.

"He did the job with great zeal, at least feigned great zeal," Ed says. "It was interesting to note that after he retired, any time he was needed he could be very often found in a poolroom."

John Smith was in Hugh Sam Holtzclaw's poolroom in Stanford years ago when Oscar Camenisch, a Lincoln County dairy farmer, bet someone $5 that he could eat a dozen eggs. Asked how he wanted his eggs cooked, Oscar said he didn't. He broke 12 eggs into a glass, stirred them up, drank them down, and asked if anyone else wanted $5 worth.

MARCH 2015

From dirt court to the Olympics

K enny Davis fell in love early—with basketball.

As youngsters, he and his brother, Ralph, inspired by the Kentucky Wildcat games they listened to on the radio, bought a basketball and rim at the Western Auto store in Monticello, and then cleared blackberry briars and a thorn tree to carve out a dirt court on their family's hillside farm in Wayne County.

Hardwood history would sprout on that small, uneven plot of land.

When Kenny shot his first layup in fifth grade PE class at Walker Elementary—and realized how easy it was to dribble a ball on a level floor—he was hopelessly hooked.

In the years that followed, he was rarely without a basketball. His mother claimed he slept with one, and he often dribbled a basketball while riding his bike. When school was out on snow days, he'd find a way into town and force open a window or door to get into the gym.

By his junior year at Wayne County High, the name Kenny Davis was being whispered in the same breath as such Monticello and Wayne County basketball legends as Jack Upchurch, Gene Pendleton and Don Frye. He led Kentucky high school scoring during the 1965-66 season, and poured in 61 points in one game.

Davis went on to become a three-time All-America guard at Georgetown College, where he scored a record 965 points as a sophomore; he is Georgetown's all-time scoring leader and was the first Kentucky college player in history to score 3,000 points.

In 1971, the 6-foot-1 Davis was drafted by the New York Knicks of the NBA and the Carolina Cougars of the ABA, but passed up both in hopes of making the 1972 U.S. Olympic team. He was team captain of the 12 chosen from among 59 who tried out.

The 1972 Munich, West Germany, Summer Olympics are remembered most for the terrorist attack on the Israeli Olympic team. But many remember those games as the year when the Russians "stole" the gold medal from the U.S. during the closing seconds of a bizarre basketball game in which they repeatedly got away with breaking international rules to win by one point.

Davis and his teammates did not show up to receive the silver medal that year, and have steadfastly refused to accept it in the more than four decades since.

In fact, Davis, 66, who had a successful 40-year career as a representative for Converse athletic shoes, has stipulated in his will that none of his family is ever to accept his silver medal. The entire story is contained in Gary P. West's excellent book about Kenny's life, *Better than Gold.*

Davis and his wife, Rita, live on a farm in the Garrard County community of Paint Lick and are members of Inter-County Energy Cooperative. Does he still shoot basketball?

"No, it's been some time," he chuckles. "I've got a goal here on our patio, but I've lowered it for my grandkids."

SEPTEMBER 2017
From hitchhiker to world champion

Y ou never know when the ride of a lifetime might appear just around the next curve on destiny's highway.

Ask Frank Smith of rural Bullitt County who, as a teenager in the fall of 1965, was hitchhiking down U.S. Highway 150 to his home in Bardstown after a visit with his grandmother in Louisville. He had no car, and hitchhiking was more common in those days.

Smith caught a ride with two couples from Nelson County whose acquaintance was to forever change his life.

Chuck and Barbara Crume and David and Bobbie Hall were on their way home to Bardstown from an archery shoot in Louisville, and though they had never met, Barbara recognized Smith as being a student at Saint Catharine College, which she attended. At the couples' invitation, he met them a few days later at the local archery range.

Ironically, his only other exposure to the bow and arrow had been in sixth grade when, at Conservation Camp, he earned every patch except the archery patch—for which he failed to qualify.

Now, at 18, with a little instruction, he fell in love with archery, and a few months later, after a chance encounter, fell in love with a girl named Sharon, a sister to Barbara Crume. As of November, they will have been happily married for 49 years.

Not only had a random ride as a hitchhiker helped him find the love of his life, but he would realize years later that it put him on the road to a world archery championship that he might never have dreamed possible.

He'd won several state archery titles in the early years, then spent six years fishing the Fishing League Worldwide pro-bass tournament trail as a co-angler with the likes of pro anglers Jimmy Houston, Roland Martin and Kevin VanDam. He served as a state representative for seven years and held numerous leadership positions with the Jaycees, Red Cross, and other civic and charitable organizations.

After early retirement from General Electric in 1997, Smith took up archery again and won a string of eight national championships in the bow hunter freestyle limited senior or veteran's divisions: three outdoor field championships, three indoor national championships and two International Field Archery Association titles.

After capturing his division's 2015 National Field Archery championship in Pennsylvania, he was chosen as one of six members of the American team in the International Field Archery Association Championship in Australia in September 2016.

The American team finished second, but Smith, now 70, a longtime member of Salt River Electric cooperative, won the World Championship in his division—veteran's bow hunter freestyle limited—using a compound bow with pin sights, finger pulls (instead of a trigger release) and a bow hunter setup, shooting 112 arrows at 28 targets per round at distances up to 80 yards.

And to think it all began more than 50 years ago when two couples he'd never met gave a teenage boy from Bardstown the ride of his life.

MAY 2018

All-star memories

Even now, Carl Howell of Hodgenville remembers how sweet it was to open a fresh pack of baseball cards in the late 1950s and lift a new lineup of major leaguers from beneath a pink slab of sugar-dusted bubble gum.

Young Carl was a devoted fan of Milwaukee Braves power hitter Joe Adcock. Like Adcock, Carl was a right-handed first baseman.

"He was everything that I admired in a player; I wore his number, 9, and always wanted to be like Joe Adcock."

Although often overshadowed by teammates Hank Aaron and Eddie Matthews, Adcock was a star in his own right. He'd hammered four home runs and a double in one game against the Brooklyn Dodgers at Ebbets Field in 1954 and played on the 1957 World Series Champion Braves team that beat the Yankees.

When he was 15, in 1957, Carl's most memorable present on Christmas morning was a baseball signed by Adcock. His father had sent a letter, along with a baseball and a $5 bill, asking Adcock if he'd be so kind as to personalize the ball for "one of his biggest fans." Adcock signed the ball and sent back a warmly-worded, hand-written note thanking Carl's father, and explaining that he'd given the $5 to the March of Dimes.

Many baseball cards listed the player's hometown on the back, and Carl and his best friend, Terry Sandidge, wrote to scores of players in the off-season, asking for autographs. They never sent a penny, but most players answered with a signed postcard that resembled a larger version of their baseball card, sometimes with a message on the back.

Carl's request to all-star Wally Moon, then of the St. Louis Cardinals, was answered with a photo of the player and a letter from Wally's father, saying that Wally was away at spring training and would be pleased that Carl was a fan.

"I am proud of him as a ballplayer, but more proud that he is a good Christian boy," the letter said. "Best of luck to you and keep pulling for the Cardinals. Sincerely, H. A. Moon."

The letter has taken its place among hundreds of other cherished mementoes from 1950s-era baseball stars Ted Williams, Willie Mays, Stan Musial, Hank Aaron and a long list of others.

Carl, a longtime member of Nolin RECC, went on to play baseball for Campbellsville College, earn a law degree from the University of Kentucky, graduate from the FBI Academy, and serve as an FBI special agent in New York before finally moving home to Hodgenville to practice law.

By that time, most of his friends' baseball cards had been lost or thrown away, while Carl's survived at his LaRue County homeplace and are now his treasured keepsakes from one of baseball's greatest generations.

Of course, the bubble would eventually burst. They don't put bubble gum inside baseball cards anymore. And they sure don't make many players who answer kids' letters.

FEBRUARY 2019

Team nicknames

A friend asked a while back if I'd ever been to the small community of
Sunfish in Edmonson County, and if I knew the nickname of their
basketball team back when Sunfish still had a high school.

They were the "Perches," he said.

Sunfish High, which closed in 1959, is among the many small high
schools with great team nicknames that existed in the years before school
consolidation—when hundreds of communities had their own high schools
and nearly all had a basketball team.

The Kentucky High School Athletic Association has only scant information
on that era, but researcher Jeff Bridgeman has compiled a 768-page *Kentucky
High School Basketball Encyclopedia, 100th Anniversary Edition* (Acclaim Press)
that's a virtual gold mine of Kentucky high school hardwood history from the
early days to the present, including team nicknames.

A few good nicknames, like the Somerset Briar Jumpers and Bracken
County Polar Bears, are still in use. But gone are the Locust "Squirrels" from
Carroll County, the Great Crossing "Apes" from Scott, the Lincoln "Tarzans"
in Middlesboro, Harrodsburg's West Side "Scalpers," Floyd County's Wayland
"Wasps" and Henry County's Smithfield "Peacocks."

Bridgeman, whose father played for Monticello during the 1930s, works as a computer specialist, but spent 11 years in his spare time assembling records of many all-but-forgotten high school teams, such as Hardin County's Cecilia "Mules"—who only lasted one season in 1931-32, Henry County's Franklinton "Diplomats," the Edward B. Davis "Mud Turtles" of Scott County, the Flat Creek "Lumberjacks" of Clay, Friendship "Quakers" of Caldwell, Marion's "Blue Terrors" from Crittenden, the Fulton County "Pilots" from Hickman and the Hamilton "Farmers" of Boone.

Any number of small high schools in those days had no gyms and practiced on dirt or asphalt courts.

"The state champion in 1929 was Heath down by Paducah, and they didn't have an indoor court until 1937," Bridgeman recalls.

So it was not unusual for teams such as Laurel's Hazel Green "Bullfrogs," Pike's Hellier "Hellcats," Hart's Horse Cave "Cave Men," Webster's Onton "Aeroplanes," or the Parmleysville "Flying Feet" from Wayne County to learn their dribbles and drives the hard way.

Girls teams usually took the same nicknames as the boys back then, with occasional modifications such as the Horse Cave "Cavegirls."

Bridgeman found a picture of a girls team from Murray High School in 1910 in which the players were wearing long white dresses.

"I thought, 'this must be a formal picture.' But come to find out that's what they played in. Because, in the same year, UK had a girls basketball team, and they were wearing the same outfits, and they had a picture of them playing on the court ... then all of a sudden I guess they decided to go with the bloomers."

My how uniforms and team nicknames have changed!

But somewhere out there, I'm guessing there may still be a Nicholasville "Tarantula," Mayking "Red Fox," Van Lear "Bank Mule," Morganfield "Guerilla" or Worthville "Hoot Owl" with enough great stories to take us into double overtime.

OCTOBER 2021

100-year-old upset

A 3-foot-high inscription, "C6 H0," in fading white paint on the corner of an old campus building at Centre College marks a glorious chapter in the Danville school's sports history—100 years ago.

On the afternoon of October 29, 1921, in Cambridge, Massachusetts, the Centre "Praying Colonels" from the central Kentucky school with a student enrollment of 262 beat the reigning Rose Bowl Champion Harvard University Crimson 6-0 in what *The New York Times* called, "arguably the upset of the century in college football."

Undefeated Harvard—boasting four national championships over the previous 10 seasons —seemed nearly invincible. Centre, though unbeaten, was starting four freshmen linemen and seemed hopelessly outmanned. Most of the Colonels played both offense and defense, and star quarterback Alvin "Bo" McMillin said, "You had to get nearly killed to have a substitute sent in." Then there was "Red" Roberts, the Centre standout who played without a helmet!

Their coach, "Uncle Charlie" Moran of Horse Cave, a professional baseball umpire in the summer, was a tough but much-loved taskmaster.

Centre had Kentucky players from Somerset, Springfield, Mayfield, Owensboro, Lawrenceburg, Harrodsburg, Lexington, Louisville and Newport and others from Texas, Arkansas, Louisiana and Ohio.

A scrapbook of news clippings that Centre lineman Col. George Chinn passed on to his grandson, Howard "Buddy" Howells of Harrodsburg, relates how Centre had been beaten by Harvard 31-14 in 1920, but played such an outstanding game that Harvard's captain offered Centre's McMillin the game ball. Bo replied, "I'd rather come back and earn it by winning."

The return battle that autumn afternoon a year later in Cambridge is legendary. Besides McMillin and Roberts, Centre started Norris Armstrong, Tom Bartlett, Ben Cregor, Minos Gordy, Bill James, George Jones, Ed Kubale, Bill Shadoan and Terry Snoddy—with Herb Covington, Dick Gibson, Frank Rubarth and John Tanner in reserve.

A smug headline in the *Boston Globe* had read, "Centre Doesn't Worry Harvard." But after 45 minutes of brutal play, Centre led 6-0. Robert W. Robertson Jr.'s book, *The Wonder Team*, in a virtual play-by-play of the game, quotes *Boston Post* writer Howard Reynolds as saying the third quarter was the greatest quarter of football he'd ever seen.

When the game ended with a 6-0 Centre victory, a gruff referee turned to McMillin with the football, and said, "Mr. McMillin, here is your ball."

Soon, buildings all over Danville and beyond were emblazoned with "C6 H0" in paint or whitewash—which 100 years have since erased. But retired Danville businessman Gary T. Gibson and Danville native Thomas Isaac of Lawrenceburg believe that, with a little help, one inscription has survived.

The victorious Colonels would have passed right by the original after exiting the train to a throng of delirious fans back in Danville and making their way up West Walnut Street where—on the corner of the old building for a century now—someone has kept repainting the score, "C6 H0."

JANUARY 2022

Great moments in sports

The old basketball resting on a cluttered shelf in the garage must be at least 40 years old. It still holds most of the same air that fueled its first dribbles and drives when our oldest son took it to the barn and began shooting baskets early one Christmas morning when he was a kid.

I can still hear the rattle of the rim that hung just inside the barn door, and I can see him climbing over the cattle feed trough to retrieve the ball when it bounced out of bounds. Below the Wilson Sporting Goods logo on the weather-beaten ball one of our boys had inscribed, in black felt-tipped marker, "NCAA" in large, uneven letters.

Rediscovering the old basketball brought warm memories of some of our family's great moments in sports. On many winter nights, "the middle room" in what then was our aged two-story farmhouse became a basketball court for our three sons and daughter. All they needed for a game was any kind of ball (even a rolled-up towel) and something resembling a goal, usually a metal coat hanger bent into a hoop and hung over the door. The kids themselves handled all the play-by-play and officiating as they played, stopping only to argue about bad calls. Often, there were post-game interviews.

Looking back, I have almost no memory of how many points or runs any of them ever scored in organized sports, but nearly perfect recall of what I now realize were the great moments.

When our middle son suited up for youth football we knew his future on the gridiron wasn't promising after he apologized to an opposing lineman whom he'd leveled during a blocking play.

Early in his rookie year of Little League baseball, his mother noticed him sliding into a base when there was no reason to slide. She asked him about it after the game and he said, "Well, when the coach put me in he said, 'Go out there and get that uniform dirty!'"

Then there was the time he came to bat carrying in his pocket a heavy paperweight with a four-leaf clover inside—for good luck.

Maybe it runs in the family. In a T-ball game years later, one of our grandsons ran the bases with his hand in his pocket. When his dad asked why, he pulled out a plastic sheriff's badge and said, "I was afraid I might lose this."

Finally, one of my favorite moments in sports was shared by a T-ball coach who remembered talking to a new team of wide-eyed rookies about their base running.

"When someone hits the ball and you're on base," the coach told them, "just watch Dave. He'll tell you when to run."

The coach said he realized he'd forgotten to introduce his assistant coach when a little boy in the back raised his hand and asked:

"Who's Dave?"

Goat Man, page 206

VII

Stories and Reflections

FEBRUARY 2011

Finding the heart of a good story

"Never so still has winter stood …" wrote George O'Neil on what might have been a gray, early February day many decades past.

Yet a silver lining gleams in February's darkest clouds through the poet's artful placement of those few simple words. Such is the power of this time of year to inspire good writing.

If you have ever wanted to be a wordsmith, February in Kentucky is a perfect time and place to begin.

Perhaps no other month is so wonderfully suited for the quiet introspection needed to transform our thoughts into poetry, a short story or even the beginning of a novel.

Cupid must have slipped Valentine's Day into the heart of February, knowing it would be the ideal time for composing love notes.

You may never have entertained thoughts of writing professionally, but maybe you should consider compiling a collection of your life's stories and observations for posterity. Many years from now, one of your children or grandchildren, or even a researcher, might consider them a treasure.

These snow-clouded days and frozen nights should not all be wasted reading pages of someone else's writings, whose stories may not be nearly as interesting as yours. Nor should they be squandered on television shows that, I once heard it said, "allow us to remain stupid without finding it dull." No, a few hours of these dwindling winter days should be used for drawing dividends on your own experiences.

So I suggest you find a cozy corner—like the one I'm sitting in now—and just start writing.

Use your heart instead of your brain in the beginning. You can fix the punctuation and spelling later. If your hands are too unsteady or your fingers too twisted to write, ask a friend to help you record your stories.

If you think your life has been dull and colorless, go back to those magical childhood dreams of what you hoped life would be, and start at the beginning. Trust me, a story will emerge.

You may want to write long letters to your children, or short stories about the happiest or saddest or most unbelievable days of your life: your funniest or proudest moments, your most profound regrets, or life lessons you'd most like to impart to others. This Valentine's Day, write a story about the love of your life.

Remember always that the heart of a good story lies in vivid details. You don't need big words, but you will often need to use your most distant, tiny memories of senses and emotions to bring the reader to a time and place, and, maybe if you are lucky, into your soul for an instant.

If you aren't in the mood to write, search your bookshelves for an author whose work is inspiring, and read until the spirit moves you.

Often, it only takes a few words, such as, "Never so still has winter stood ..."

MAY 2011

Miss Edna's call forwarding

M any years before today's fancy smartphones, Glendale had "Miss Edna." I never drive through the scenic Hardin County railroad village that I don't recall a story told by Frank Hatfield, who grew up there during the 1940s.

In 1953, Hatfield, who now lives in Bullitt County, was serving as a plane captain aboard the aircraft carrier USS Tarawa in the Caribbean, when the Red Cross notified him that his mother was ill and he needed to contact his father back in Glendale.

Frank was flown from the ship to Guantanamo Bay Naval Base in Cuba to make the call.

When he told a telephone operator in Miami that he was trying to reach Fred Hatfield, the operator asked for the phone number.

"I don't have a number," he told her. "All I know is that our ring is three shorts."

He had never much needed to remember the number, he said, because in those days his family mostly wrote letters instead of making expensive long-distance calls.

When the operator tersely informed him that she'd need a number to make the connection, Hatfield assured her that if she could reach Glendale, the call could be completed.

He heard operators connecting in Atlanta and later in Elizabethtown, then heard the familiar voice of switchboard operator Miss Edna Crowe say "Glendale."

The Miami operator explained that she had a call for a Mr. Fred Hatfield, but that she didn't have a number.

"Edna didn't hesitate," Frank remembers. "She said, 'Well, he's not at home. Just a minute, I'll see if I can find him.'"

Hatfield and the surprised Miami operator held on as Miss Edna, in a manner befitting Sarah, the mythical Mayberry operator on *The Andy Griffith Show*, began ringing phones around Glendale.

"I heard her ring up, and A.T. Hayes said, 'Hardware,' and she said, 'Is Freddy in there?' A.T. said, 'No, I think he's over at Hardy's.' So she rings up Hardy's general store, and Floyd Hardy answered and said, 'Yeah, he's right here.'"

The Glendale telephone exchange was located upstairs in the post office building where Miss Edna and her spinster sister, Mary Alice, the other operator, could look out on Main Street and see most of what was going on in town.

Folks often alerted Mary Alice or Edna when they planned visits around the county, in case anyone needed to reach them. Many farmers called the sisters when they had cattle and hogs to ship to market, so the operators could relay word to livestock haulers.

Hatfield, a former superintendent of Bullitt County Schools and executive director of the Kentucky Retired Teachers Association, said he recounted the story for an AT&T consultant some years ago.

"She was explaining to me how call forwarding worked and how much it was, and I said, 'Well, shoot, we had call forwarding in Glendale in the 1950s, and didn't pay for it.'"

AUGUST 2011

Barefoot Ben

Every year about Kentucky State Fair time, someone reminds me of the old man with a long white beard and walking stick who trudged barefoot to the state fair each year to watch the World Championship Horse Show.

If you were at the fair during the 1960s or before, you may have seen him there, or walking along a highway en route, always with the legs of his bib overalls rolled up to mid-calf.

Charles Ben Wilson was born in Anderson County in 1883 and grew up on a farm in the Alton Station community near Lawrenceburg.

He loved horses and could recite the pedigree of most prominent Saddlebreds.

Ben, a lifelong bachelor, was eccentric to be sure, but neighbors regarded him as intelligent, hardworking and not without financial resources. Many children in the community believed he was Santa Claus.

Passing motorists who gave him a ride were treated to bits of his homespun philosophy, such as this quip from 1956:

"This is the day of unlimited knowledge, but not unlimited wisdom. Our trouble is that our wisdom hasn't kept pace with our knowledge."

Ben naturally became a favorite subject for the media, and he seemed to enjoy the celebrity. He made a cameo appearance in the motion picture *The Flim-Flam Man*, some scenes of which were filmed around Lawrenceburg in the mid-1960s.

Richard Crutcher, John Allen Perry and Kenneth Smith, all of Anderson County, still remember seeing Ben often walking barefoot—sometimes even through the snow, according to Perry and Smith—and Smith recalls once seeing him barefoot in the middle of a briar patch picking blackberries.

Crutcher overheard Ben mumbling as he walked barefoot past his place on the hot asphalt highway one summer, "Suffer, xxxx feet, suffer."

During the state fair, Ben usually slept in a tack room or in the cattle barn.

One night while window-shopping along Fourth Street in Louisville, he was arrested for loitering. But influential horsemen and cattlemen raised such a fuss that a judge apologized to Ben for the arrest and dropped the charges.

Ben had gone West during his younger days, working as a sheepherder in Idaho and at a logging camp in Washington state.

Asked what people out West thought of the way he dressed, he snapped, "The people out West minded their own business."

After his death in August 1969 at a home for the elderly near Lawrenceburg, a letter dated 1956 was found among his personal papers. It stated: "I want to congratulate you on your performance as Santa Claus for the kids the other day. You made a good one."

A few years ago, an elderly state fair goer whom I had never met stopped me at the fair and said he wanted to give me something.

It was an envelope filled with small black-and-white Kodak snapshots of Ben Wilson in his bib overalls—barefoot, of course.

The state fair is not the same without Ben.

JUNE 2012

Remember the day that Dad…

One afternoon when I was home alone I brought in the old wet-dry vacuum from the garage to remove from a corner of the fireplace a small clump of soot that must have fallen from the chimney. That's when it all started.

I turned on the vacuum, stuck the nozzle into the soot, and waited for it to disappear.

It vanished from the fireplace all right, but instantly reappeared pretty much all over the living room. The vac somehow blew part of the soot backward all over my left leg and shoe, the coffee table, the floor, part of a bookcase, a leather sofa that had been brown, and even the wall.

When my wife, Jackie, came home, I was cleaning up as best I could, still partially covered with soot.

"Why can't you just take a nap when I'm gone?" she asked.

That ugly episode triggered painful flashbacks of other unforgettable blunders.

Years ago when no one was home, I tried to warm up some leftover sloppy joes but somehow got distracted, went outdoors, and left the sloppy joes on the burner.

By the time I smelled smoke, the sloppy joes mix was more like (to borrow from a well-known movie title) Sloppy Joes Versus the Volcano. The house had to be fumigated.

Then there was the Christmas that I got a metal detector and could not wait to give it a try.

About dusk on a Sunday, I was searching in the side yard near the edge of the woods, along a small creek, hoping to unearth some long-lost relic of the past, maybe a blacksmith's tool, or a toy tractor from the 1930s.

I was almost ready to give up when the metal detector treasure alarm sounded a long, loud, joyous beeeeeeeeeep!

"Whoa!" I thought. "This is something big." After more beeping, I determined that the mysterious underground object, whatever it was, was slender and long. At this point I'm thinking Civil War sword, or maybe even a musket.

Light was fading fast and the old long-handled shovel wasn't moving enough dirt, so I fetched a grubbing hoe from the garage and went to work. After a few furious swings, I found the object that had set off the metal detector. It appeared to be a piece of cable.

I was still pondering the discovery when someone yelled out the door that the television had just gone off. It turned out that my "treasure" was the television cable, and I had stopped the CBS network's famous stopwatch in mid-tick.

Our four children gleefully remember the embarrassing incident as "the night Dad dug up *60 Minutes*."

I still have the metal detector, but rarely used it after that night. It is stored in the garage, right next to a soot-covered wet-dry vac.

I need a nap.

SEPTEMBER 2012

Runaway washing machine

Our back page story in May about Myrtle Rickman Cooper's memories of her mother's clotheslines and washdays (page 14) set Wayne Baxter of Taylor County to remembering an incident from his boyhood on the farm back in Monroe County.

"On a Sunday morning in about 1950, this old truck that we usually went to church in wouldn't start," Baxter says. "So my dad decided that we could drive the old World War II army surplus dump truck that we used out on the farm, that we could get to church in it, though it didn't have a sign of a brake." You see, Wayne's father, Bazz, thought he had mastered the art of driving the old dump truck without brakes. He simply geared down the vehicle to a virtual crawl in its lowest gear—"bulldog"—then turned off the ignition to stop.

That Sunday's trip on the back roads to Mill Creek Baptist Church, about 13 miles from the Cumberland River farm, was uneventful. Wayne, who was 9, and his two brothers, Kirk and Warner, were riding in the back of the truck, and their mother, Della, and 7 year-old sister, Loretta, were in the cab with Bazz. Returning from church, they stopped at Wayne's grandparents' place.

"It just so happened that the REA had turned the electric on out there on the ridge about that time, and my grandparents didn't need their old gasoline-powered washing machine any more, because they had a new electric model.

So they gave us their old washing machine, and somehow they got that big old metal machine up in the back of that dump truck, with my two brothers and me up in there with it."

Rural electricity had not yet reached the Baxter place, so the brothers were excited at the prospect of having a gasoline-powered washer that would spare them the chore of helping their mother wash clothes on a washboard.

During the trip home, their conversation turned to how to get the washing machine started. And after some discussion, Warner, the oldest and most mechanically gifted, allowed as how he could start it. Just as his father was gearing down to begin a half-mile long descent down a steep hill, Warner kick-started the washer, and the loud roar so startled Bazz that he missed the bulldog gear at a crucial time, then couldn't force the old truck into second or even third.

The boys hung on for dear life and the unrestrained washing machine bounced around the truck bed, still running full throttle, as the old Army dump truck careened down the hill for several hundred feet. At the last minute, Wayne's mother quietly suggested the hand-operated emergency brake, and Bazz wrestled the truck to a stop. To the boys' surprise, their father didn't punish them. But he did ask Warner why in the world he started the washer.

Warner's reply: "It seemed like a good idea at the time."

JUNE 2013

Goat Man

Time was when a mellow June evening drew many Kentucky families to the front porch at twilight—where conversation usually drifted from events of the day to grander subjects.

These included any number of tall tales, legends of supernatural mysteries and stories about unusual characters.

Among my 1950s memories of some of these colorful personalities was a kind of nomadic herdsman known to some Kentuckians as the "Goat Man."

This swarthy, bearded wanderer passed through our rural Lincoln County community on U.S. Highway 150 one or two summers during the 1950s—with maybe 20 or more goats pulling a rickety steel-wheeled wagon bedecked with all manner of artifacts: license plates from many states, lanterns, mirrors, hubcaps, bottles and other curiosities.

Two or three stray goats were discovered roaming about the countryside one year after he departed.

In 1988, after I mentioned the Goat Man in a newspaper column, some 50 readers recalled their encounters with him and his goat caravan from the mid-1930s through the 1950s.

A woman who saw him in Christian County when she was a child said he was heading south down U.S. Highway 41 in the fall; that he was a medium-sized, hairy man, with bare feet like leather. She said he wore overalls with no shirt, and with one strap over his shoulder.

A Louisville woman found a 1953 newspaper clipping about his visit to Jefferson County with 27 goats. The story said he sat in an aluminum chair that had been an airplane seat, sipping coffee from a quart jar.

Allen Grider of Barren County wrote that when the Goat Man passed through Russell County in 1950 or '51, his lead goat was named "Woosie."

The late Jodie Hall of Grayson County said the Goat Man once told him that when he came to a hill, the goats following the wagon would push. It was true, declared Bill Mack of Shelby County, who said he once witnessed the trailing goats pushing on command as he followed the Goat Man through the hills of Tennessee.

Later, Joe Dorris, a beloved columnist for the Hopkinsville *New Era*, got word that the Goat Man, Charles "Ches" McCartney, was living at a nursing home in Macon, Georgia, where he'd been taken after losing some toes to frostbite in 1987. He died in late 1998 and was believed to be age 97.

A Macon newspaper reported that McCartney took to a life on the road after losing his farm in his native Iowa during the Great Depression. He sometimes returned there in the summer, but wintered on a small tract of land he owned near Macon. He claimed he had been to every state except Hawaii, and was afraid to go there because his goats might eat the grass skirts off the hula dancers.

FEBRUARY 2014

Returned with regrets

When I recently crossed paths with Carol Ann Hunter, whom I'd not seen in years, she mentioned that she still has her pennies.

Years ago, she had shared with me the story of how her stolen pennies had been returned nearly three decades after they disappeared.

When she was 16 and lived in the Henry County community of Campbellsburg, a cardboard coin book containing 70 pennies was stolen from a little shop where she sold costume jewelry and clothing next door to her parents' home.

She'd opened the shop partly with savings from the paper route she started at age 10. The pennies, in their book, disappeared from a desk where she kept a few personal items.

Twenty-eight years later, she was married with two sons and living in Oldham County when her mother, Margaret Hayden, then living in New Castle, phoned to say she'd received in the mail a package with no return address, marked simply: "Attention Carol Ann."

Inside were the missing pennies, still in the correct slots.

Carol Ann wishes that whoever returned the pennies had written an anonymous note explaining his or her thoughts. The collection will always be more special, she says, because of its story.

Another random act of regret concerns the wallet stolen from Virginia Broyles' purse when she worked at a Danville drugstore in 1945. It mysteriously showed up on a street in Danville and was turned in at police headquarters in January 1990—44 years after it disappeared.

A few dollars and some gas and sugar ration stamps were missing, but Virginia's 1945 driver's license, Social Security card and photos, including those of her husband, W.G., dressed in his Navy uniform, were intact.

Then there was the discovery that Clay and Velma Lykins of Jefferson County made just before Christmas in 1992, when they stepped onto their porch one night to turn off the Christmas lights and saw a large object wrapped in plastic at the end of their driveway.

Under the plastic was the wicker rocking chair that had been stolen from their porch 18 years earlier, and this note:

To whom this may concern: Approximately 13 to 17 years ago my husband stole this wicker rocking chair from the porch of this house. I am ashamed of this behavior and am returning this stolen item. I have since been divorced from my husband and have since been "born again." My life has completely changed and I want to undo any wrongdoing to the best of my ability. I know this chair is not in the same condition as when it was stolen and I apologize. I now live in another state, Tennessee, and am rarely in this vicinity. I realize the cowardly fashion in which I am returning this, but the reason is obvious. I will not bother you again. Please forgive us. Sincerely.

The rocker was placed in a bedroom—along with the letter—which itself became a treasured keepsake.

SEPTEMBER 2014

Garage treasure

A few days ago I found myself in a no man's land we call our garage, trying to "clean up."

The project began in front of an antique mantle bought years ago from a trader who claimed it had originally belonged to famous Kentucky frontiersman Col. John Floyd. I didn't believe a word of his story, but enjoyed the tale so much that I bought the mantle anyway.

It now was bedecked with an assortment of old tobacco pegs, a small black bear made from Kentucky coal, a shaving brush that a mountaineer fashioned from a corn shuck, a wooden object I can't identify, a dusty trophy with a Holstein cow on top that I won in a dairy festival cow-milking contest years ago, a SpongeBob nightlight, a heavy horseshoe marked "first iron 1972" from a foundry in Cynthiana, a small plastic man, and on and on.

Groping through a tangle of drop cords to a forest of 25 or more fishing rods, a minnow seine, 4 1/2 pairs of hip waders, three scooters and six golf bags to a place where I could see daylight, I heard the voice of one of our sons, Wesley, somewhere behind me, offering to help.

Naturally, I thanked him, but knew that, given half a chance, he'd consign nearly everything in the garage to next week's trash pickup.

You see, I was thinking *Antiques Road Show*. He was thinking *Hoarders*. It wouldn't have surprised me if he'd had a psychologist waiting in the laundry room to offer me counseling.

Up for discussion: a like-new work glove with no mate in sight, a light fixture with cast-iron horse heads from the demolished original Executive Inn across from the state fairgrounds, a pressure washer with a defective pressure hose, a large sign marked "Winchester School of Culture, Beauty and Design," and a yard-sale find of an old Wollensak tape recorder on which our middle son, Joe, made his first audition tape and got a job at a local radio station at age 14. He's now a morning DJ in Seattle, and I'm stuck with the tape recorder that no longer has a power cord.

Atop an aged gumball machine was a boy's 1950s vintage, green-and-gold plastic Hutch brand football helmet with a faded autograph decal that reads "Babe Parilli," a University of Kentucky All-American. Who in their right mind would throw that away? Then I found a long-play Col. Harland Sanders Christmas album, with a cover picture of the Colonel dressed in a Santa suit.

After much discussion we decided to throw away the work glove and a defective extension cord, and to move three of the golf bags and the pressure washer closer to the door, and then rearrange everything else. We finished all except one corner before I had to leave early.

The next-door neighbors were having a garage sale.

JULY 2015

Cruising with Rosa

E ven after all these years, the thought of her still brings a smile.

I met Rosa Lora Greenwell only once many summers ago. She was 86, but her laughter was ageless, and she loved sharing stories of her misadventures.

She had once owned a dress and uniform shop in Louisville, she told me, and had always seemed prone to blunders that, while not so funny at the time, grew more comical when viewed through life's rearview mirror.

Her husband, Marvin, was a Louisville motorcycle policeman in the 1930s and had a siren installed on his personal car, which was the vehicle for the following story:

Rosa was driving the car when she and four women friends arrived at Harrodsburg one day in the 1930s, hoping to catch a glimpse of President Franklin D. Roosevelt during his brief visit to the Mercer County seat.

"We all had on hats and gloves and were dressed nice," she said.

Soon after arriving in town, they came upon a street barricade with soldiers standing guard.

"I still don't know why I pulled that siren," she recalled, "but they dropped the rope, and I just rolled over it and went on."

The women immediately found themselves in the middle of FDR's small welcoming parade. In fact, right behind FDR's car, as Rosa remembered. Her sister in the back warned the women not to "act guilty," as she began waving and smiling to the adoring crowd.

They kept up appearances until Rosa finally nosed the car into an alley, where the women all breathed a sigh of relief and had a good laugh. Back home in Louisville, Rosa's husband failed to see the humor in the incident and removed the siren from the car. But the ladies in their hats and gloves would ride again.

Being one of the few women in her lodge group who drove, Rosa often gave other women a ride to the meetings. One winter night she was driving another woman's car—a two-door model—with four passengers. When the meeting ended, a light snow had left streets a bit slippery.

The car wouldn't budge, so all of the able-bodied women got out to push. Then Rosa noticed that the emergency brake was on and released it. Those pushing all fell flat, and Rosa said one woman's hat with big ribbons on it tumbled off her head and went rolling into the street.

They finally got underway, but later, as Rosa was letting one lady out on the driver's side, the car was knocked into gear and lurched forward, the open door striking a fire hydrant. Rosa slammed on the brake and the disheveled women in the back seat again went to their knees, and the big hat with the ribbons came flying into the front seat.

Rosa heard one woman mutter that if she ever got home alive she'd never ride with Rosa Greenwell again.

AUGUST 2016

Competition in blue

Musical genius George Gershwin gave us *Rhapsody in Blue*, but Jeanne Kemper is composing her own version of that classic in culinary competition at the Kentucky State Fair.

Over the past three decades, she has won enough blue ribbons with her kitchen creations to have tempted perhaps even Gershwin to put down his music and go for dessert.

This year she is preparing 52 entries in the candy division. Yes, you read it correctly. Fifty-two.

She and her husband, Leonard, retired longtime Shelby County dairy and tobacco farmers—members of Shelby Energy Cooperative—must make two trips to the fair's exhibition wings in their SUV loaded with contest entries of cakes, pies, honey cookery and other delicacies.

Luckily, they've never had an accident, but they did have to slam on the brakes suddenly one year, and Jeanne cringed when some of the cakes slid forward. No damage was done.

Then there was the year she forgot the delivery deadline for contest entries and wound up with 16 pies that were ineligible.

"We ate a lot of pie," Leonard recalls.

Looking back, Jeanne is sure that she inherited her competitive spirit from her late father, W.T. White. But it was her mother Carroll's willingness to let her experiment with cooking as a youngster that gave her confidence in the kitchen.

"No matter how bad I did, she always found something good to say about it," Jeanne remembers.

When she was about 10 and in 4-H, Jeanne had won a blue ribbon for her biscuits at the Shelby County Fair, but for years, into her 30s, she showed three-gaited Saddlebred pleasure horses. Then, with two children and more work to do on the farm, she finally gave up riding and entered some of her cakes in the state fair in hopes of winning a sweepstakes.

Large sweepstakes rosettes are awarded to those who accumulate the most points for ribbons in a given class—with blue ribbons earning the most points. Winners of sweepstakes must wait four years to re-enter the same class in which they've won. Jeanne failed on her first attempt, but won the sweepstakes for her cakes in 1985.

"I just thought I had won Miss U.S.A.," she says. "It couldn't have been any better."

Since then, she has won 51 coveted sweepstakes rosettes, 16 since 2008. She has long since lost count of the total blue ribbons she has brought home, but they number close to 500.

"Jeanne is a really nice person, but when it comes to competition, she is a true competitor," says Kentucky State Fair Culinary Department Superintendent Stephen Lee.

Jeanne admits that she is now aiming for 60 sweepstakes rosettes, but adds, "It's not just about the ribbons for me. I have so many lasting friends that I never would have had without entering, and I've just learned so much from people. I've told some of them they're better than winning a blue ribbon."

OCTOBER 2017

The perils of youth

O n a night long ago, in a yesterday fondly remembered by some as "the 1950s," there lived a mediocre singer/guitar player by the name of George Gobel. Short in stature and musical talent, perhaps, but a giant of comedy.

George was so profoundly ordinary that he would have stood out in a parade of ordinary people.

His hair was closely cropped in a crew cut. His suits and ties were exceedingly plain, and he had a lonesome look about him—even when he was happy.

America fell in love with his dry wit and deadpan delivery. "If it weren't for electricity we'd all be watching television by candlelight," he told us. And, "Did you ever get the feeling that the world is a tuxedo and you're a pair of brown shoes?"

NBC gave Lonesome George his own weekly TV show. And in the small Bourbon County village of North Middletown, the Garrison brothers, Everett and Jim, and their friends Steve and Horace Bacon, all mostly in their early teens, were huge fans who rarely missed one of George's shows.

As darkness fell that evening, one of the boys mentioned it was almost time for George Gobel. Seeing as how Steve Bacon was at his parents' house across town, the other three decided to ride their bikes to the Bacon place so they could all watch the show together.

They had to ride past a neighbor's house where a small dog usually chased the bikes and nipped at their heels. He was probably harmless, Everett remembers, but the boys always tried to outrun the dog by pedaling faster past the neighbor's.

In the darkness, as time drew near for *The George Gobel Show*, Steve Bacon—unaware that the other three were speeding toward him—was racing across town hoping to join George Gobel, his brother and their friends at their house.

Without lights on the bikes, and with the street light out near where the dog lived, the boys were guided mostly by instinct as they sped along the same quiet street toward one another.

The three heard the dog barking before they reached the house where he lived, but would learn much too late that he was barking at Steve who, at that moment, was racing past in their direction.

Seconds later, Everett, who was behind the others, heard the crash of metal against metal, and saw a shower of sparks as Steve and Jim's bikes collided nearly head-on.

Jim was knocked out and suffered a mild concussion; Steve was still conscious, but badly rattled and thrown from his bike.

Perhaps worse yet, they missed George Gobel, who went on the air that evening unaware that he had caused a dangerous bike wreck among four of his most ardent fans.

The dog—having witnessed the wreck—trotted happily back home, satisfied that he had kept the street safe for another night.

NOVEMBER 2017

Cake wars?

Our thoughts this time of year often drift through a dreamy haze of Thanksgivings past to cherished memories of family gatherings and fireside conversations; cozy kitchens rich with the aroma of yeast rolls, ham, turkey, puddings, pies and cakes.

Ninety-six-year-old Geneva Logsdon's memory ventures back some 70 years to a "chocolate cake incident" in her mother-in-law's kitchen.

Her son, David Logsdon of Louisville, told me a few months ago that his mother has been troubled by the episode since the late 1940s.

A few days later, I visited her assisted living residence to hear the story firsthand. She was trim and alert, with a ready smile and a warm handshake. I wouldn't have guessed her to be 96.

Yes, her son was right, she said. She still harbors bad feelings over the chocolate cake incident after seven decades. She sometimes dreams about it.

You see, Geneva and her sister-in-law, Ruthie, never got along very well. They weren't exactly enemies, but minor differences had dulled their friendship.

On what Geneva believes was a Thanksgiving Day in the mid- to late 1940s she and Ruthie—who passed away many years ago—arrived at Geneva's mother-in-law's, Granny Logsdon's in Bullitt County, each with a chocolate cake they had baked. Geneva loved chocolate and had found the cake recipe on the back of a Hershey's cocoa can. She'd already baked one cake from the recipe for a gathering of her Sunday School class, and had gotten wonderful reviews.

At Granny Logsdon's, she and Ruthie both placed their chocolate cakes side by side atop what in those days was called an "icebox," a forerunner of the refrigerator.

Geneva showed me exactly how the cakes were situated, using the top of a small chest in her room to explain that Ruthie's cake would have been to my left facing the chest, and hers to the right.

She described in detail where the women were standing in the kitchen, Ruthie on the right side of the icebox—near Geneva's cake.

During the course of conversation, Geneva said she looked away for a moment and, "KABOOP!" She turned to see her beautiful chocolate cake splattered on the floor, and the antique cake plate that belonged to Granny Logsdon, broken.

Worse yet, Geneva is nearly certain she saw a wry smile on Ruthie's face. And it's been bothering her all these years.

"Somebody helped that cake come off of there," Geneva told me.

Would Ruthie have done such a thing? "Yep," she whispered.

She never again ate any of Ruthie's cakes.

"I've had to ask the good Lord to forgive me for how I was thinking about her ... if I've been wrong to accuse Ruthie," she said. "I think it's helped me to get a little bit of it out of my system."

She asked if I thought she was making too much of the chocolate cake incident.

It's hard to say, Mrs. Logsdon. I'd have to taste your cake to be sure.

JANUARY 2018

Life lessons

While searching a cluttered file for a long-lost photograph a while back, I came across a misplaced letter from a Grayson County Middle School teacher, dated January 1995.

I was a newspaper columnist in those days and had written a column about life lessons. The teacher, Donna White, had shared the article with her seventh-grade language arts students, then asked them to list some of their own life lessons to send me.

Having just written on the subject, I must have decided to save their notes for use in another column sometime down the road. But I didn't intend it to be 22 years!

Though most of the "kids" would be in their mid-30s now, some of the lessons they wrote about when they were 12 or 13 are worth sharing, even at this late date:

Randy Swift wrote: *I have learned not to copy somebody's work, because the answers are not right.*

Sean Mangan: *I have learned never to lie down in the yard if you have a dog... or drink orange juice after you've brushed your teeth.*

Landon Hayes: *I've learned that when you have trees in your way at the golf course, aim to hit the one in your way and you will probably miss it.*

Jamie Decker: *I have learned never to trust your big brother when he says, "Go ahead and jump, I'll catch you."*

Kevin Logsdon and Jonathan McKinney offered lessons that will be appreciated by our safety-conscious Kentucky Electric Cooperatives staff and membership. Kevin's lesson: *I have learned that you should never put a raw egg in the microwave while it's still in the shell.*

Jonathan's lesson, no doubt learned at a much earlier age: *The plug-in outlets are not the place to keep your pennies and dimes.*

Shannon Reedy: *No matter what your brother says, don't trust him when he says you can laugh and eat pudding at the same time.*

Jo Williams: *The best way to win a fight is not to throw the first punch. If it's only a minor skirmish, just sit there and grin at them. It drives most bullies crazy. However, be ready to duck if necessary.*

Cara Brooks: *I have learned that if you live on a farm and you don't want to open and shut the gates, you should ride in the middle of the pick-up.*

Fortunately, I was able to find their retired teacher, Donna White, a member of Warren RECC, who still lives in Grayson County and is an animal rescue volunteer with the Grayson County Humane Society. She remembered the "life lessons" letter and was surprised to hear that I was reprinting excerpts in this month's back page.

But she didn't remember that she had ended her 1995 note to me with a life lesson of her own: *"I've learned that there is nothing like having two college degrees and being stumped by a 2-year-old's 'why?'"*

221

APRIL 2018

Tellin' tales

Kentucky could use a few more storytellers.

Yes, we still have some good ones left, but their ranks are thinning much too fast.

When county courthouses throughout the state shooed away the whittlers, and country stores began to vanish—taking with them the liars' benches; when fast food chains replaced the mom and pop diners, and self-service gas stations put the old service stations out of business; when small town pool halls, barber shops, feed mills and other fine loafing places closed their doors, the storytellers' primary habitat was lost.

One by one, storytellers, too, have faded away, and with them many stories worth remembering.

I am thinking just now of the late Waller Sam Denny, a native of Lancaster in Garrard County and a masterful storyteller, who used to tell me about the time four boys in his class at Lancaster High School decided during their lunch hour to drive out to Dix River, not far from town, and wash a car that belonged to one of the boys.

Washing a car in a nearby river or creek was a common practice during the 1940s and '50s in rural Kentucky.

The boys stayed a little too long that day and were late getting back to school, but had made up a tale to tell the teacher—an attractive young woman whom they adored—that they had had a flat tire on the way back from washing the car.

"Well, you're lucky," the teacher told them. "All you've missed is a pop quiz, and you have plenty of time left to take it. I want each of you to go to a different corner of the room with pencil and paper and face the wall.

"There is only one question on this quiz: Which tire went flat?"

The late James Gillenwater of Barren County, a lawyer and former "gavel and gravel" county judge, told me about one of his many courtroom encounters with attorney J. Paul Carter of Monroe County.

He said Carter once told a jury, "Now James Gillenwater is going to tell you that you shouldn't find this man guilty because it's only circumstantial evidence. I want to tell you members of the jury that circumstantial evidence is the best kind there is.

"Suppose you're out on a snowy morning hunting rabbits and you see ol' Brer Rabbit's tracks and follow him through the snow to a hollow log. You see the tracks where he went in, and no tracks coming out the other end. Now, where is Brer Rabbit? That's circumstantial evidence."

Finally, Ray Brown, who used to be a barber in Elizabethtown and was a great storyteller, remembered Weed Chelf, a long-ago town constable who wouldn't drive a car, but often hitchhiked to and from other communities to bring back prisoners—handcuffed to himself! Weed is said to have once hitched a ride in the back of a pickup truck, whose driver he wrote a ticket for speeding when the ride ended.

OCTOBER 2019

The wingless plane

The senior class at Chandlers Chapel High School in northern Logan County had only 10 students in the year 1950. All boys.

One of them was Jim Lockhart, now 86, who lives a few miles west of Russellville and who told me this story about his school days:

"The main roads were gravel with potholes, and the secondary roads were mud with mud holes. The closest blacktopped road was 5 miles away. Outdoor toilets, and we had a well."

But Chandlers High had something that even most big-city schools did not have: An airplane.

The school principal and geometry teacher, Mitchell Watkins, had been an engineer at Republic Aviation in Evansville, Indiana, which built thousands of P-47 Thunderbolt fighter planes during World War II.

One day on a field trip to the airport in Bowling Green, Watkins and the boys saw an old single engine airplane for sale for $125. It may have been an early Piper, but Lockhart's not sure. Anyway, Watkins bought the plane, hauled it back to the school on a farm trailer and began teaching an aeronautics course to the boys.

"We didn't take it up in the air, but we'd take the wings off and drive it up and down those gravel roads. We all took turns, you know," recalls Lockhart, a longtime member of Pennyrile Electric.

The plane, a "tail dragger," had to be started by cranking the propeller. It had two seats, one behind the other. The boys had goggles that they sometimes wore during outings with the plane along the dusty roads—where they sometimes got up to 35 miles an hour. None had a pilot's license, but of course they never got off the ground except in their minds.

The sight of a plane fuselage roaring past on a country road often caused a bit of a stir. The story goes that a woman's hens were so traumatized that they stopped laying, and that a farmer's bull was so rattled that he left home for two weeks.

"One Sunday afternoon, me and two other boys spray-painted that thing with a fly-spray gun," Lockhart says. "We painted it black. That was the only color paint we had."

Oddly enough, none of the 10 boys chose to go into aviation after graduation.

Lockhart, whose family owned a farm and a service station in Russellville, eventually took over the family business and later owned a chain of service stations in central Florida. He now is retired to his farms in Logan County.

One morning on Russellville radio station WRUS-AM, a two-star general was a guest on morning talk show host Don Neagle's popular *Feedback* program, and Lockhart called in to share with him the amusing story of the aeronautics course and the wingless airplane from his high school days.

The general—somewhat surprised that none of the boys had joined the Air Corps after high school—asked Lockhart why.

Jim's memorable answer: "I guess we were overqualified."

FEBRUARY 2020

Written memories

There is a place in Hardin County where memories of a lifetime find rest in words on the written page.

"I tell them not to worry about spelling and punctuation, just to get their stories in writing," says Jo Bailey, a retired Elizabethtown High School English teacher, who now encourages writing among residents of RobinBrooke Senior Living in Elizabethtown.

After retirement, Bailey was invited to do a poetry reading for women at the senior living community, and soon she was urging them to write their own poems and stories.

One of their topics was to write about their last boyfriend. Another project they called "Our Lives in Fives," beginning with recollections of their first five years of childhood and continuing, in five-year increments, to the present.

Barbara Mills mused about looking forward to hand-me-down clothes from her older half-sister, Donna, when they were children during the 1940s. She later wrote poignantly about how she was tempted to skip writing about the painful years when she and her late husband, Charles, a pharmacist, learned that their young daughter, Susan, had an inoperable brain tumor, which took her life at age 13.

Former middle school art teacher Mary Carolyn "Micki" Howell, who was born in 1927, remembered her first stick of Dentyne chewing gum, and that she was almost 5 before she tasted ice cream. She wrote about the Great Depression and her mother, a registered nurse, working for 25 cents an hour on the second shift at a General Motors plant in Anderson, Indiana.

Through their pens and computer keyboards flow testaments of their faith, their happiest and saddest moments, their love for their children and grandchildren, and indelible snippets of everyday life in decades past.

"In the fall of 2015, I rode with Charles in the combine out at the Bush Farm," wrote Ernestine Nall. "The moon was shining, and the colors of the corn outshone the moon. It was so bright and beautiful. I was just the 'farm mother,' and it was very enjoyable just to be riding with my son."

Occasionally, Bailey, a consumer-member of Nolin RECC, shares her own writings with the group. Her following poem, Love at 56, seems appropriate for Valentine's Day this month:

A-h-h love, what is it?
Please define it for me if you can. If you dare.
Tell me it is long-lasting and comfortable and secure.
Tell me it is what I have.

Don't let me think it is just young, moist kisses,
A quickening of breath, a skipping of a heartbeat
For a moment when the loved one is first seen.

Tell me love is holding a newborn. Love is sometimes
Standing in a cemetery...together. Tell me
Love is forever. Oh, do not tell me that love was only
That brief frenzy of hands and faces seeking to possess.

*For God's sake, don't tell me **that** was love.*
Not now. Not now.

NOVEMBER 2020

A loser

E mbarrassing though it may be, it's time to admit that I am a loser. Not just one of the everyday "what-did-I-do-with-the-TV-remote" variety. I'm in the advanced class.

I've lost track of when it all started and have lost count of all the small items that have disappeared. These include a natural pearl, a little larger than a BB, from an oyster that I bit down on in a restaurant many years ago. A jeweler who examined it guessed that, in its raw form, it might be worth $60. But as a conversation piece it was priceless. I doubt that I had it more than a month before it vanished.

Then there was the silver bullet (made of plastic) that the late actor Clayton Moore, aka The Lone Ranger, gave me when I met him back in the 1970s. It was lost quicker than you could say, "Hi-Yo Silver, away!"

Gone, too, is an autographed picture of Evil Knievel, signed by the motorcycle daredevil during an interview before one of his death defying jumps.

Several years ago, I was asked to speak to a Christmas dinner for employees and their families at a manufacturing company in southern Kentucky. I placed my notes on the lectern at the head table when I began, offered a few words of greeting to the crowd, then glanced back down at the notes—which were gone!

Knowing that they had slipped off the lectern and onto the floor, I glanced around as best I could while continuing to speak, but they were nowhere in sight. So I gave up and winged it.

When the event was over, I looked under the tables, under the lectern and anywhere else I could think of, but my notes were nowhere to be found. I was speechless.

It gets better … or worse.

My wife Jackie's wedding ring, which was removed at a Lexington hospital when she had surgery for a shoulder injury, was handed to me in a zip-close plastic bag when she was dismissed. I tucked it into one of my pockets, and we haven't seen it since.

A few months later, after mowing the yard, I lost my glasses between when I parked the riding mower in the garage and when I got back inside the house. I searched the shrubbery several times—once with a metal detector—walked over the yard about four times, sorted through the recycling, rearranged one whole side of the garage, and searched the zero-turn mower. But the glasses have never been found.

If there is a "Losers' Support Group," I'll bet the discussions are interesting.

A scuba diver from Somerset told me several years ago that he had been called to Lake Cumberland to search for everything from diamond rings and other expensive jewelry, to sunken houseboats and runabouts—and many sets of false teeth that boaters and swimmers have lost while coughing or sneezing.

Right then is when I realized that I'm not even qualified to wear dentures.

JANUARY 2021
"Before I die"

The words are hard to miss—"Before I die," in 12-inch white letters atop two large blackboards on the façade of an antiques shop in the heart of Nelson County's historic Bloomfield.

Beneath those words on each board are more than 40 lined spaces in which visitors are invited to complete the thought, "Before I die, I want to…" A chalk box is attached to each board.

From my first notice of the boards several years ago, there was little doubt they were the work of Linda Bruckheimer, a novelist, photographer, preservationist and entrepreneur who, along with her husband, Hollywood producer Jerry Bruckheimer, owns Walnut Groves Farms just north of town. Beyond her interest in antiques and primitives, she is also fond of curiosities, quirky objects and roadside whimsy.

She says she'd like to take credit for the "Before I die" project, but she saw the original in New Orleans years ago when local artist Candy Chang stenciled the words "Before I die…" on the wall of an abandoned house that she turned into a giant chalkboard in remembrance of the unfulfilled life of a friend who died unexpectedly.

Her desire was to encourage people to confront life and death, and to share their thoughts with others, Bruckheimer tells me. It became an unlikely catalyst that encouraged expression and uplifted the community. Copies of the wall were soon popping up in other places, and now number in the thousands.

When in the fall of 2013 Bruckheimer had the "Before I die..." boards installed in front of the antiques shop that bears the name of her paternal great-grandmother, Nettie Jarvis, she was unsure what type of response they might evoke.

"But within hours, both boards were full, and we were out of chalk!"

All these years later, people are still coming from near and far to add entries to the ever-changing list. One of the questions Bruckheimer is most often asked about Bloomfield is: "Is Bloomfield the town with the 'Before I die...' sign?"

Some visitors to the chalkboards list places they hope to travel; many want to see world peace or leave political statements. Some want to study a foreign language, lose weight or "marry the girl I saw in the parking lot at Walmart." One even wanted "to marry Mrs. Bruckheimer!"

In the end, the overwhelming goal left in most messages is not the mountain they want to climb or the Cadillac they want to own, Bruckheimer says. They want to be a better wife, husband, parent, friend, person. "They want to serve God, and of course, there is winning the lottery," she says.

When I stopped to look at the chalkboards a while back, a few of the entries that caught my eye were, "I want to make peace with all those I've hurt or wronged" and "I want to raise my family, be a role model father and own a zero turn mower."

Then there was the wish, apparently left by a child: "I want to have a mommy."

MARCH 2021
The ex-files

While clearing the contents of two old file cabinets back in the winter, I began browsing through some of the scores of outdated folders filled mostly with letters (those things we wrote to each other before emails, texts and tweets). There were clippings, photos and scraps of paper marked with names and phone numbers of readers who may have sent me story ideas many years ago when, in another life, I wrote a newspaper column three days a week about anything I found interesting between the Big Sandy and the Mississippi.

Often in a rush, I tucked ideas inside folders, scribbling a subject on the tabs, until finally there were eight drawers of file folders ranging literally from A to Z. I never got around to writing many of the stories, and most folders hadn't been opened for decades. Their contents include everything from "lost mines and buried treasures," to "feuds," "ghosts," "folk medicine," the "James Gang" and "strange but true."

An Associated Press clipping from 1983 and datelined "Corbin, KY," told of a 38-year-old man from Lebanon, Ohio, who survived an accidental plunge over Cumberland Falls. Larry Slaughter had waded into the water about 100 yards above the falls to save his 5-year-old son who slipped from a rock into the river. His son made it safely to the bank, but Slaughter was swept away and fell 68 feet over the falls. He said he held his nose, prayed to see his family again and "felt this suspended feeling like I wasn't existing anymore … like I was suspended in air." He was treated at a local hospital for a leg bruise after what he described as "a miracle."

Two folders were filled with tales about "madstones." These rare and mysterious, usually porous, small stones—often said to have been found in the stomachs of deer—were used in the late 1800s and early 1900s to treat victims of bites by rabid animals. Numerous eyewitnesses and bite victims claimed that the stones, when soaked in warm milk, would take on a spongy texture and stick to the wound, presumably drawing out the poison. The few madstones that still exist are now treasured relics.

Another file yielded a photo of an alligator snapping turtle found in the Ohio River near Owensboro and estimated to be about 150 years old; some notes on the "shoo-fly plant" that repels flies; stories of snakes, scorpions and cougars; and eyewitness accounts of the New Madrid Earthquake of 1811.

Then there was "Beckham County," the only Kentucky county ever to be abolished. Created by the legislature in 1904 and named for then-governor J.C.W. Beckham, it lasted only a few weeks before being dissolved by the state Court of Appeals.

Finally, here was a quote from a leading magazine that an arthritis specialist had said many arthritis sufferers can in fact feel it in their bones when rain is on the way.

I guess my grandmother was right!

SEPTEMBER 2021

Rockabilly revival

Muhlenberg County has never been short on notable musicians: Among them, Ike Everly and his sons, the Everly Brothers, Merle Travis of *Sixteen Tons*, a virtual Who's Who of other legendary "thumbpickers," and singer-songwriter Bill Harlan—whose fascinating story is a ballad in the making.

Born in 1937 to a family of music lovers, Harlan grew up in the coal mining community of Cleaton, across the street from the Baptist church where his father, a miner, was choir leader.

After the Everly family relocated to Iowa, Don and Phil spent summers with relatives in Muhlenberg County, and countless hours with their close friend, Billy Harlan, who is the same age as Don. Thinking back on those summers, Harlan recalls, "it doesn't seem like we ever slept."

Hours were spent playing guitar and the bass fiddle or writing songs, and Harlan, along with his friends Royce Morgan and Dave Rich, performed with a band called The Melody Hands. His senior year at Drakesboro High School, 1955, he wrote a song called, *My Fate is in Your Hands*. Although it would fail to get much airplay, it was recorded by Grand Ole Opry star "Hawkshaw" Hawkins, who died with Patsy Cline and others in a plane crash.

In 1957, Harlan joined singer Jim Reeves' band as the upright bass player and was on tour with Reeves in Europe when the Everlys' first hit, *Bye Bye Love,* was released.

To his disappointment, four songs he later recorded with RCA and Brunswick either weren't released or failed to make the charts. So needing a rest from the music business, he went west, worked in the aerospace industry, studied computer science and had a successful corporate career.

Fast forward more than 50 years. Now remarried, Harlan was living back in Muhlenberg County in comfortable retirement with his wife, Ann, when a Las Vegas promoter asked him to appear at a rockabilly music festival in Vegas.

Those songs he'd written and recorded in the late '50s may not have been hits in the U.S., he was told, but the master recordings had been bought by a German-based record company and released as part of a rockabilly compilation in Europe, where the songs *I Wanna Bop, School House Rock, This Lonely Man,* and *Teen Jean Jive,* had been popular among European fans for several years.

"And I didn't find out about it till 2012."

Long story short, Harlan, now 84, has since made four appearances at the Vegas festival and has been to Europe three times, with tour stops in England, Austria, Germany, France, Italy, Switzerland, Sweden and Belgium. Beyond any financial reward has been the sight of fans of his music waiting in line for photos and autographs after all these years.

"I guess there's a lot of 'what might have been,'" says Harlan, "but I'm thankful for what I have."

JANUARY 2023

Tradio

Some of my favorite radio programs when I travel across Kentucky are the live call-in shows where listeners offer items for sale or trade, and post want ads, all for free.

Their catchy names include *Tradio, Dial & Deal, Trading Post, Swap Shop, General Store* and *Adcaster*, to name a few. Most are morning broadcasts hosted by popular air personalities who preside over a virtual yard sale of the airwaves—with a few smiles thrown in.

Paul Priest of WXBC-FM in Hardinsburg remembered a man calling *Bargain Barn* with a set of used tires for sale.

"He said, 'I'll tell you what, Paul, I'll sell 'em right, and I'll guarantee they've never been squalled.'"

Chrissy Parrish, a Clinton County consumer-member of South Kentucky RECC and longtime host of WANY-FM's *Trading Post* in Albany, tells of a caller wanting to trade some chickens for a motorcycle. And Trish Stacy, host of *Free Market* on WSGS in Hazard, recalls a man wanting to sell 722 boxes of Kraft deluxe macaroni and cheese, "or, I would trade them for a good rooster."

Don Johnson of WKYR-FM in Burkesville was once given an item for his *Swap Shop* program while paying respects during a funeral visitation.

Dave Cox, a former manager of WIRV in Irvine, now retired to Florida and hosting a Saturday morning program on a Flagler Beach radio station, remembers a call from a woman on WIRV's *Trading Post* who was looking to find a good home for her late husband's artificial leg. But Dave's most memorable call came from a woman who was trying to locate the owner of an Irvine High School class ring from 1965, which had been found nine years earlier.

Inside the ring were the initials "DEC."

"That's *my* ring!" Dave yelled.

He had looked for it every place he could think of—and even searched his yard with a metal detector—after losing it while erecting a ham radio antenna in his backyard. He'd gone to WIRV to pick up some tools, but was sure he'd lost the ring in the yard.

The caller, who lived in Irvine, explained that she didn't have his ring, but that it was in the possession of her daughter, Jeannie Farwell, in Walton, just over 100 miles away.

She said a retired couple from another state had moved to Irvine many years before, and, after the wife died, her husband briefly took a room downtown where he found the ring near a curb. The man soon moved to Detroit and later passed away.

His daughter, who lived in Ohio, found the ring in a cigar box while sorting through his keepsakes. Her friend, who was there when the ring was discovered, was acquainted with Jeannie Farwell, and knew that Jeannie was originally from Irvine.

Jeannie told her mother back in Irvine, and her mother called the *Trading Post* at WIRV—having no idea that the ring's owner would answer the phone!

Mystery of Mandy, page 252

VIII

Folklore

Ball of fire

Among Kentucky's many chilling tales of unexplained phenomena are scores of eyewitness accounts by reliable people who have vowed that they were true.

So it was with this strange happening in western Kentucky, described to me years ago by the man who saw it.

The late J.F. Hankins said that when the incident occurred in the mid-1950s, he owned a 256-acre farm off U.S. Highway 231 in northern Ohio County, about halfway between Hartford and Owensboro. From his farmhouse, he could look across the bottomlands to Barnett Creek.

He had recently discovered a few of his tools missing and was keeping a close eye on his barns and other outbuildings, hoping to catch the thief.

One October night, he heard his dog, Boots, barking and looked out to see a bright light moving around one of the barns. Then it circled a second barn before heading toward an unoccupied tenant house.

Hankins was sure that the light was a gas lantern. It was three or four feet off the ground and bobbing along about the speed of someone at a brisk walk.

He grabbed his double-barreled 12-gauge shotgun, loaded it with No. 6 buckshot, and slipped away toward the road along the creek where he guessed the thief had parked his car and would be bound to come past him. Sure enough, the light came down the road toward where Hankins was hiding in the edge of a cornfield with his fearless watchdog at his side.

When it was about 30 yards away, Hankins stepped out of the cornfield, leveled his shotgun at the light, and yelled, "Hold it right there!" Boots lunged forward and started to bark, then stopped dead still.

The light was still coming toward them, but there was no one holding it.

It was just a "bluish-like" ball of fire about 16 inches through, Hankins said. It illuminated the roadbed beneath it, the edge of the cornfield and the surrounding roadside.

Hankins stood frozen in his tracks as Boots lay whimpering at his feet and the ball of light approached them. Just before it reached them, Hankins said, it turned and passed through a gate, then turned and followed a fence beside a cow path leading to the creek.

When it reached the creek, it turned again and moved down the middle of the creek channel, bobbing up and down 3 to 4 feet above the water.

Hankins said he watched in disbelief as the light "followed every little crook and turn" of the stream, until it went out of sight under a bridge on the county road.

He has always wondered what would have happened if he had fired his shotgun at the light.

Hunters later told him that they had seen a similar light while hunting at night in the creek bottoms.

Was it swamp gas? Maybe. But a university researcher later said that the description of the light matched no naturally produced gas source.

OCTOBER 2012

Star-struck

Many years ago, as darkness fell over a fishing hole on Dix River in Lincoln County, I was walking back to my old Jeep when I heard a strange, loud, crackling noise, similar to an arc welder, and noticed a greenish glow on the surrounding landscape. I looked up just in time to see a greenish fireball, low in the sky, falling toward Earth. Then the crackling noise ceased and the light vanished. In my late teens at the time, I knew no one to call, but I have mentioned the incident to nearly every geologist and astronomer whose path I have crossed since then.

The sighting was typical of a rare, close encounter with a meteor, said Richard Gelderman, professor of physics and astronomy and director of the Hardin Planetarium at Western Kentucky University. Many such events may go unrecorded or unnoticed, but some have made news in Kentucky over the years.

Stony or metallic objects from collisions in the asteroid belt are called meteors as they are falling, but meteorites after they strike Earth. Since the mid-1800s at least 27 documented meteorites have been found in Kentucky, from Pike County in the east to Calloway, Marshall and Livingston counties in the west.

In September 1990, a 3.3-pound meteorite fell through the porch roof of a Pike County couple near the community of Burnwell. The Smithsonian

Institution in Washington, D.C., acquired the stone.

The rare Calloway County meteorite that fell in September 1950 contained several amino acids not found on Earth. Grains from the 28 pounds of meteorite fragments recovered 9 miles east of Murray have helped scientists study the age of the Milky Way galaxy.

People in seven states observed a spectacular meteorite that fell in Bath County in November 1902. The largest chunk, weighing 178 pounds, was recovered the following spring.

Other meteorites have been found in Allen County, Barren, Bullitt, Carroll, at two sites in Casey County, in Christian, Clark, Franklin, Grant, Harrison, Jefferson, Kenton, Lincoln, Metcalfe, Nelson, Oldham, Simpson, Taylor, Trimble, Wayne and Whitley. They are each described in a publication available from the Kentucky Geological Survey called *Space Visitors in Kentucky: Meteorites and Meteorite Impact Sites in Kentucky*, by William D. Ehmann and Warren H. Anderson.

Anderson, a research geologist and minerals expert with the Kentucky Geological Survey, says many of the meteorites found in the state are now in major museums around the world. But some small ones from the William Ehmann collection are displayed in the foyer of the Mining and Minerals Resources building on the University of Kentucky campus.

Anderson has examined hundreds of rock and mineral specimens brought to the university over the years by people who believed they had a meteorite, only to find out that meteorites are very rare, and most rocks found in Kentucky are naturally occurring iron oxides or carbonates such as hematite, limonite, magnetite, siderite or a piece of pig iron, iron slag found in the vicinity of one of Kentucky's many historic iron smelting sites.

APRIL 2013

Rattlesnake crossing

Just when I thought I'd heard all the strange snake stories in Kentucky, my old friend Bill Mardis—Pulaski County's beloved sage of field, stream and folklore—asked if I'd ever been to the "rattlesnake crossing" in eastern Pulaski County.

No, there isn't a "rattlesnake crossing" road sign, he said, but the rattler crossing on Bolthouse Ridge Road, not far from the Rockcastle River and near the Rockcastle County line, is for real.

Eighty-three-year-old Delmer Turner, a lifelong resident who killed a timber rattler a few months ago with a hand ax, said his grandfather, who was born in 1880, told him that the rattlesnake crossing was there when he was a child.

Most everyone in the nearby communities of Acorn, Ano and surrounding countryside is aware of the crossing, and most can share a snake story. Adams Grocery at Acorn has pictures on its wall of many timber rattlers that have been killed.

Delmer Turner's son, Tommy, a Republican state representative who lives close by, says the rattlers generally cross the road along a half-mile stretch, but that the majority seem to prefer crossing at a narrow point no longer than 100 yards. The once-gravel, now chip-seal, road was bordered by scattered woods and farmland some years back, but now the roadsides are reclaimed strip-mine land with a few scattered pines.

If the rattlers have been affected by any of the changes, it is not apparent. George Arthur, who owns land at the far end of the road, believes there may be even more rattlers crossing now than in the past. He knows of one man who killed nine on the road last summer. Copperheads are also present, but appear to have no particular crossing pattern.

Tommy Turner, whose son and grandson killed three timber rattlers on the road one night last summer, says it seems that most of the snakes that cross in the spring are going in the opposite direction of those crossing in the fall.

His great-grandpa had a theory that many of the rattlers had been born among the rocky outcroppings of Baker Hollow on one side of the road and that they returned to hibernate. He may have been right.

John MacGregor, a herpetologist with the Kentucky Department of Fish and Wildlife Resources who knows as much as anyone about Kentucky reptiles, says the rattlers may be migrating to hibernate, or they might have a "rookery," or breeding colony, nearby that would likely be in a dry, sunny place with large boulders. Six female timber rattlers could give birth to as many as 40 or 50 young.

Turner, an avid hunter, could recall no rattlesnake bites to people in recent years, but he remembers a hunting dog being bitten several years ago and dying before it could be brought out of the woods.

In the warmer months, people often drive Bolthouse Ridge Road just before dark, looking for rattlers.

OCTOBER 2013

Ghost tree

Anyone who has walked a country lane after dark knows how moonlight on the landscape can create ghostly images from fence posts, bushes and stumps.

Yet some insist that a frightening form that seemed to emerge from a large beech tree beside a country road in the Trammel community of western Allen County years ago was more than imaginary.

The story goes that in the early to mid-1800s a man was hanged from the tree by vigilantes. Later, some passersby began seeing frightening apparitions there. Details of the lynching have dimmed with time, but tales of what older people still call "the hainted beech" live on.

Leroy Henson, longtime pastor of the Martha's Chapel General Baptist Church in Warren County and a member of Warren Rural Electric Cooperative, says that his grandfather, Henry Howell, was among the trusted members of the community who saw the ghost.

Howell, a deeply religious man who was a deacon and school board member, died in 1944, several months before Henson was born. But Henson's grandmother, Deimer Howell, told him the stories when he was a boy.

His grandfather, a farmer who also did carpentry work around the community, often came home by horse and buggy after dark on the Middle Fork Hollow

Road, now known as Mayhew Road. The large beech stood just where the road begins its descent into a long hollow.

Henson says that on several nights when his grandfather passed the tree, he would see something—sometimes in the fog-shrouded form of an animal, and at other times in human form—that would run beside the buggy.

"It would excite him, but he wouldn't just lose it, like I would have," Henson says. "On a few occasions, whatever it was would get in the buggy seat beside him and ride for a ways. The first time this happened, he didn't know what kind of an animal it was, and it was a moonlit night, and he reached over in the floor of the buggy and picked up a hatchet and threw it—and it just went through whatever this was."

Others told of an apparition in the form of a person getting on the horse behind them as they rode past the tree.

"They said it would be just a real cold feeling, kind of like a chill in the air, even in the summertime," Henson says.

Henson's own father saw a mysterious white form in the road near the tree one night in the early 1900s while returning from Franklin.

During Henson's teen years, he remembers speeding up and trying not to look while driving past the tree. One night when he was about 17 and his car broke down, he walked through fields and briar patches to avoid the haunted beech.

The old tree is now long gone, but there are several young beeches growing within a few feet of where it stood.

OCTOBER 2015

The Lone Oak ghost

Hidden behind the stately Greek Revival columns of one of Hopkinsville's historic homes is a haunting legacy of ghostly tales involving one of the home's long-ago occupants.

Jimmie Courtney Hickman Thompson died in 1919, but many, including the home's current owner, Jim Coursey, are sure that her ghost still roams the large two-story residence—known as Lone Oak—which dates to 1835.

Coursey, who retired from a successful career in interior architecture and design in New York City, had heard numerous stories about the ghost long before he bought the place and began renovation in 2006.

Although it is now a house museum shown by appointment, Lone Oak was for several years an upscale dining establishment. Back then the ghost was blamed for rearranging glassware during the night, occasionally pulling someone's hair, and once for shoving a female restaurant employee down the cellar stairs.

"She doesn't like women in general, and redheads and blondes in particular," says Coursey.

He doesn't know how Jimmie Thompson died, but local lore has it that her later life was not a happy one, a story perhaps enriched by the belief that her spirit still haunts the place.

Neighbors tell of seeing a woman in the window when no one is known to be in the house.

Coursey says he feels her presence when someone she doesn't like is a guest. He was once awakened in the dead of night with the pale apparition of a slender, slim-faced woman—resembling a photograph he had seen of Jimmie Thompson—staring down at him from in front of a window. The form materialized, he says, from what he might best describe as the snowy white dots that were often seen on the screens of old black-and-white televisions.

One night when a man and two women were house guests, he heard a woman's voice loudly calling, "Jim! Jim!" But both women were sound asleep and said they had not called.

His dogs, a bull terrier and a Rottweiler, won't go into what was Jimmie's upstairs bedroom, and despite new wiring throughout the house, lights have never worked properly in her room.

"In the wintertime the dogs stay up in my bedroom with the door closed, and I have come home to find one of the dogs downstairs and all the doors shut between upstairs and down—and he would be just shaking like a leaf. Once, she locked the bull terrier out on the balcony upstairs and it took me about three quarters of an hour to find him."

Some years ago, five Christmas presents mysteriously disappeared from under the Christmas tree, and a thorough search of the house turned up nothing.

"I went upstairs to her room and had a little chat and said, 'I want those things put back.'" Coursey says. "The next morning, there they were under the Christmas tree."

JUNE 2016

Words of the day

A while back, Steve Russell, of the Windsor community in Casey County, noticed in the local newspaper an interesting phrase used in a traffic accident report.

A man whose car had rear-ended another vehicle told police that the driver in front of him "just bowed up and stopped."

Steve, a member of South Kentucky RECC, wondered if I was familiar with the term.

"Bowed up" is one of many unusual phrases dwindling into obscurity and possible extinction.

The Dictionary of American Regional English or *DARE* (Harvard University Press), which lists thousands of such terms—including many used in different regions of Kentucky—offers multiple definitions of bowed up: "standing up to someone," "turning mean," and a usage most familiar to me as a central Kentucky farm boy: "When cattle in winter stopped and humped their backs up, they were said to 'bow up.'"

A University of Wisconsin researcher, gathering information for the massive dictionary, once called to ask if I had heard of a bettywood tree.

He said the name appeared in some of Kentucky's earliest surveys in Bourbon, Bath and perhaps a few adjacent counties, and that no one seemed to know to which species the nickname referred. I'd never heard of a bettywood, but printed an inquiry in a newspaper column inviting anyone with information on the name to contact the researcher.

The current *DARE* entry for bettywood states that conclusive identification was never made, but a lengthy explanation notes that available evidence suggests that bettywood may have been a local name for a sycamore, or possibly a birch.

Among the scores of other listings used in parts of Kentucky are: airish, meaning "the weather is getting cooler," and cattywampus, the table was nice and straight until he came along and "knocked it cattywampus." (Our word for that was sigogglin').

The late Paul Dalton of Allen County wrote his master's thesis at what is now Western Kentucky University on *Elizabethan Leftovers in Allen County*, and long ago gave me a list of words and phrases that were still used occasionally in some parts of Allen County. Among them: shebang, an old Irish term for a place where liquor is sold illegally. Smidgen, archaic for "a little bit." Swivet, from Scotland, meaning "a nervous state of mind." Fair up, the clearing of clouds after a rain.

Dalton said he had found numerous words and phrases that traced beyond Shakespeare to the earlier works of Geoffrey Chaucer.

Then there is the collection of eastern Kentucky words and sayings remembered by the late Appalachian writer Verna Mae Slone of Knott County, in *How We Talked:*

Blinky, milk just beginning to sour; riddie bob, a seesaw; poor doe, gravy made with water when there was no milk; disfurnish, to sell or give away so much that you are in need yourself.

This is by no means the whole "kit and kaboodle," and I welcome your additions to the list.

Mystery of Mandy

Among Kentucky's many ghost stories, the tale of Hopkins County's "Mandy Tree" is one of the most unusual.

After more than a century, the death of Amanda (Mandy) Taylor Holloman, an attractive young African American woman, is still a mystery that might have long been forgotten were it not for the chilling appearance of her silhouette in the tree under which her body was found one morning in the summer of 1915. Margie Bowman of the Historical Society of Hopkins County recounts that Mandy was found lying near the base of a white oak tree she loved in the backyard of the home where she and her husband lived on West Broadway in Madisonville.

Incredibly, her death from a gunshot was ruled a suicide, though no weapon was found and many of her friends insisted she'd been murdered.

News accounts said a grown stepson had been in the home that morning, and had arrived late for work, but claimed he had left home just after his father. Mandy's two younger children had gone to a town spring for water a few blocks away, and reportedly found her nude body wrapped in a quilt under the tree when they returned.

In time, the property—including the white oak—passed into the hands of African Methodist Episcopal ministers H.V. and Madeline C. Taylor.

Their grandson, Ron Elliott, says his grandmother once confided to family members that she and her husband had feared, at one point, that they might be unable to make the mortgage payments and might lose the property. She said she began praying for help.

About that time, Elliott says, someone noticed that the foliage of Mandy Holloman's beloved white oak had grown into a silhouette of her likeness looking up into the heavens.

Those who had known Mandy were amazed at how much the profile resembled her facial features, hairstyle and even the high collars that she often wore.

Crowds began coming to see the Mandy Tree on nights when the moon was behind the tree's haunting silhouette. *Life* magazine published a photo of the tree, copies of which are still in the hands of some family members.

Elliott's grandmother sold refreshments to sightseers, and his father, photographer Robert Lancaster Elliott, sold picture postcards of the tree. They didn't get rich by any means, he said, but they made enough to help with the mortgage payments.

It is unclear when Mandy's profile eventually vanished from the foliage. The white oak was finally destroyed by lightning.

Perhaps in a fitting postscript to the story, a man who was remodeling the home during the 1980s discovered an old .22 caliber rifle—the possible murder weapon—hidden in a wall around a fireplace. The rifle has since been given to Mandy Holloman's great-nephew, John T. Taylor Jr. of Madisonville, who keeps it as a sad reminder of his great-aunt Mandy's unsolved death and of her haunting image in the family tree.

MARCH 2018
Capital Columbus

"**G**ood tales die hard," wrote historian Allen Anthony in his book, *Columbus, KY as the Nation's Capital: Legend or Near Reality?*

I can't remember when I first heard that the small Hickman County village of Columbus, on the banks of the Mississippi River, was once considered as the site for the capital of the United States. But if you spend much time in western Kentucky's Jackson Purchase region you'll hear the story sooner or later.

It's difficult to know exactly who started the tale in the very early 1800s, but before long, even Thomas Jefferson and James Madison were implicated.

A popular claim was that Jefferson, the nation's third president, after negotiating the 1803 Louisiana Purchase, had a "definite" plan to move the nation's capital to a more central location—said a 1949 editorial in the *Phoenix* (Arizona) *Gazette*, later quoted in the *Hickman County Gazette*.

Yet, Anthony—a retired professor of history and geography, a former resident of western Kentucky and graduate of Western Kentucky University, now living in San Antonio, Texas—says he has spoken to no one among the Jefferson scholars, from Monticello to the University of Virginia to Princeton, who has ever found documentation that Jefferson wanted to move the nation's capital to Columbus.

Historians also note that the Kentucky land now known as the Jackson

Purchase was not ceded to the U.S. by the Chickasaw Nation until 1818.

Nevertheless, the legend has refused to die. An old state historical marker at the site reads: "Columbus was proposed as the nation's capital after the War of 1812," a claim that survives on an interpretive panel at the site, and on a related website.

In early 1870, Robert Summers, editor of the *Columbus* (Kentucky) *Dispatch*, (not to be confused with the later *Columbus Hard Times*) wrote: "... and standing on this site President James Madison once said, 'here, some day, will stand the capital of the nation.'"

"Robert Summers loved to spin a tale, and this was a great story," says prominent Hickman County writer/historian John Kelly Ross of Clinton, who credits enthusiastic publishers and local real estate con artists of long ago with keeping the story alive despite no basis in fact.

"There was nothing here," says Ross. "In 1821, it was just a flat piece of land, surrounded by bluffs, that got flooded a lot. Who's going to put the capital there?"

Columbus did become a strategic site during the Civil War, when the Confederate Army mounted large cannons on the bluffs and stretched a giant chain all the way across the Mississippi River to block Union gunboats. The chain, each link of which was said to weigh 20 pounds, 5 ounces and measure 11 inches in length, soon broke from its own weight. Pieces of the chain are still on display at the site, which is now occupied by Columbus-Belmont State Park.

The massive chain may have broken, but the romantic legend of Columbus being considered for the nation's capital has proved to be all but indestructible.

JULY 2018

Tellin' tales of big cats

Just at dusk on a backwoods trail in McCreary County many years ago, Judith Hensley was stunned when what appeared to be a black panther bounded across the road in front of the jeep in which she was a passenger.

She'd been visiting friends at their weekend cabin on Parker's Mountain, and was returning home with them when the large, long-tailed animal crossed their path no more than 20 feet in front of the vehicle.

"It was an incredible thing to see that big black cat that looked like something you might see in *The Jungle Book*," she recalls. "We all saw it."

The driver, Elmer Boggs, who was the county extension agent, had already told Hensley that panthers existed in the area. She remembers that he turned to her and said, "I told you."

Hensley went on to become a teacher in her native Harlan County where she's now a columnist for the *Harlan Daily Enterprise* newspaper. But even after all these years, the memory of what she's sure was a panther sighting in the late 1970s is a continuing source of intrigue.

Her fascination with the subject was further fueled by tales about big cat sightings that she's read and heard over the years. So many that she finally decided to gather such stories for a book on the subject—not to prove or disprove the existence of mountain lions or panthers in Kentucky, but to preserve the folklore. She posted a notice on the Facebook site, Appalachian Americans, asking anyone with stories of such sightings to get in touch.

"I think I got like 330 responses, and within about 48 hours I had to take the post down because I couldn't respond to everybody who had sent a story or comment."

Some shared tales handed down by ancestors, while others related their own sightings of tawny mountain lions or black panthers. A few asked that their stories not be printed out of concern that they might be ridiculed. Many who consented to have their stories told are included in a book of about 300 pages that Hensley released on Amazon and Kindle in late spring: *Panther Tales and Woodland Encounters.*

Although Kentucky was once part of the native range of the eastern cougar, the animal has long been officially believed extinct here. State wildlife officials maintain that, while mountain lions have been confirmed in Missouri and Tennessee in recent years, there is still no credible evidence of their natural presence in Kentucky. They believe that animals recently killed or captured here were brought from outside the state.

A Michigan researcher studying alleged "black panther" sightings in western Kentucky several years ago theorized that most purported panther sightings are likely black leopards that may have been raised as pets, but released into the wild when they became unmanageable.

Hensley is already at work on Volume II.

JULY 2019

Crow call

Millions of crows have made Kentucky their home through the dim mists of time, but few have earned individual mention in a history book or talked their way into their own exhibit in a museum.

Pete accomplished both.

He was the star attraction at a hat shop in Georgetown from 1829 to 1832, or so the story goes in B.O. Gaines' *History of Scott County, Kentucky, Vol. II.* We know nothing of Pete's age, his life before he came to live at the hat shop or his early education. But if we are to believe this brief page of history, Pete was a talker with a fairly impressive vocabulary—at least for a crow.

It's long been known that some pet crows can be taught to speak, and it's assumed that the hat shop owner, Dave Adams, must have been a major influence on Pete.

Adams was an avid horse racing fan and often took Pete along to races on the edge of Georgetown. Many race starters in those frontier days simply yelled, "Go!"

Gaines tells us that one day in the excitement of the start, Pete yelled, "Go!" and was rewarded with applause. Upon discovering that he could yell "Go!" he began to shout it often around the horses, sending them on many bad starts.

He was believed to have picked up several profanities from local fishermen whose minnows he often stole from their buckets. And it's recorded that when he was thrown out of a woman's house after plucking feathers from her hat, he yelled, "Curse your soul, I'll tell George Sawyer!" George worked at the hat shop.

Some townspeople claimed that he often greeted them with, "Good morning! A cold, frosty morning!" And it was reported that a drunken wagon driver fell off the wagon into the mud and was nearly run over by his own wheels when Pete alighted on the wagon and exclaimed, "Bill, oh Bill, oh Bill!"

One man claimed that Pete said, "They haven't got as much as I could eat," when someone walked past with a basket on their way to the market.

Sadly, Pete's life was cut short when a boy who was visiting Georgetown mistook him for an ordinary crow and shot him. A small coffin was built by students at Georgetown College, and Pete was given a proper burial on the campus. The location of his grave is unknown.

There is today a permanent exhibit in Pete's honor in a back corner of the Georgetown-Scott County Museum: an animatronic, talking Pete replica that entertains museum visitors from a perch atop a post.

Retired Georgetown College Theatre and Film Studies Professor George McGee, a member of the museum board and a consumer-member of Blue Grass Energy, believes a marker should be placed somewhere on the college campus to commemorate Pete's colorful contribution to local history and folk life.

So far, the college administration has not given its approval, but McGee is not giving up hope.

MARCH 2020

The Red Bird Stone

Hidden among the cliffs, rock shelters and caves of Kentucky are mysterious chapters of lost history, chiseled in stone.

The "Red Bird Stone," a boulder estimated to weigh 25 tons or more, is among the most visible examples. It tumbled from a sandstone cliff near the Red Bird River onto State Route 66 in Clay County in 1994, and now rests under an open-air shelter in the city park of Manchester, the Clay County seat.

On its face are many markings, or petroglyphs, believed to have been left by ancient visitors whose origins continue to puzzle researchers.

Archeologists from the University of Kentucky and University of Tennessee are generally in agreement that the inscriptions—consisting largely of linear grooves—appear to be ancient Native American in origin. Still another theory by some is that the markings were the work of later native tribes during the period when the Cherokee, Shawnee and others are known to have had a presence in the region.

However, Jan Simec, a University of Tennessee archeologist who has studied numerous Cherokee sites, doesn't believe the Red Bird Stone petroglyphs were left by Cherokee or other tribes. And Simec further dismisses theories that inscriptions on the Red Bird Stone and strange markings at other sites around the region were the work of ancient explorers who ventured across the Atlantic before Columbus.

But James Burchell of the Clay County Historical Society, who, along with former Clay County Judge-Executive James Garrison, is credited with saving the Red Bird Stone from destruction, insists that the stone contains several Old World scripts, including ancient Hebrew and Greek.

Burchell, a member of Jackson Energy Cooperative, has been familiar with the markings most of his life, and had always assumed they were Native American. But two years before the 18-foot-long boulder dropped from the cliff, he sent detailed photos and descriptions of its markings to Barry Fell of Harvard University, an internationally prominent invertebrate zoologist, renowned epigrapher and author on ancient life in America.

Burchell has a letter from Fell verifying Old World inscriptions on the Red Bird Stone, accompanied by an ancient alphabet matching some of the cryptic carvings.

Fell, who died in 1994, was widely criticized by professional archeologists and anthropologists who complained that his research failed to meet their standards, but he gained immense public popularity during the 1970s and '80s with his first book, *America B.C.*, and two sequels. He theorized that Celts, Egyptians, Phoenicians and other Old World explorers found their way to North America untold centuries before Columbus, and that, when deciphered, many of the mysterious marks on rocks such as the Red Bird Stone, provide solid evidence of their presence.

Burchell is convinced that some of those ancient explorers, following rivers and streams from the Gulf to the Great Lakes, stopped to leave what they hoped would be a lasting record of their passing, etched among the cliffs and caves, and on the giant boulder that we now call the Red Bird Stone.

AUGUST 2022

Possum Trot

Even when I'm seriously lost in a jungle of backroads, the sight of a colorful place name on a highway sign always makes me feel better about not knowing which way to turn.

Three of the most memorable in Kentucky's far western Jackson Purchase region are Monkey's Eyebrow and New York in Ballard County, and Possum Trot in Marshall.

While the origins of some great place names are obscure, I'll say it again—if you look at a map of Kentucky, the part of Ballard County bordering the Ohio River resembles the profile of a monkey, with the Monkey's Eyebrow about where it should be.

New York, at the junction of state routes 286 and 802 in southern Ballard County, loses most of its place name signs to souvenir hunters, but Jackson Purchase Energy Cooperative still has a substation there that keeps the name alive. A local storekeeper with a sense of humor is believed to have come up with the name New York about 1913.

Possum Trot's history has been better preserved, thanks to Cecil Moore, a lifelong resident of the neighboring north Marshall County settlements of Little Cypress and Possum Trot. From the age of 14, Moore, now 81, has been saving the many stories he's gathered from ancestors and others in the two map-dot villages near the Cypress Creek tributary of the Tennessee River.

In the early days of Little Cypress nobody knew anything about Possum Trot, he says. But the old Calvert City road that ran through the area was then a dirt road and was often covered with so many possum tracks that it came to be known as "the possum trot," which sparked other stories.

Local resident George Lawson was heard coming down the road one night about 1900 singing, "The old gray goose laid—and the gander sot—upon the golden street of Possum Trot."

A story retold in Robert Rennick's *Kentucky Place Names* has it that locals Sol King and Buck Bolen were possum hunting along the road one night in the early 1900s when one remarked, "If we don't catch one soon, these possums are going to trot across the road and be gone."

Those and other colorful tales add spice to the book Moore is compiling from his fascinating collection of history and local lore. One chapter among the 200-plus pages will be a diary kept by Benjamin Johnson Story, a blacksmith who also operated a grain thresher and sawmill, once served as postmaster, and was a notary and railroad ticket agent. He died when struck by a train in the summer of 1929.

Moore writes of childhood train trips to carnivals at Kuttawa in neighboring Lyon County, countless personalities of yesteryear and many events dating to pioneer days. A lifelong consumer-member of Jackson Purchase Energy, he vividly recalls when his family got electricity and stopped using oil lamps after moving to the farm where he grew up and where he still lives today—between Little Cypress and Possum Trot.

Gifts of time, page 268

IX

Christmas

DECEMBER 2011

A blanket, a stone, a piece of string

"We began to make ready for Christmas."
Words from Mary Breckinridge's memories of 1925 evoke primitive snow-globe images of mule-drawn farm wagons, filled with mountain families, arriving at the unfinished "Big House" of logs that would become the home of the Frontier Nursing Service at Wendover in Leslie County.

Though the logs were still unchinked, there was warmth around the large fireplaces, and the Christmas air, sweet with the scents of baking hams and pies, mingled with the chatter of children around a mountain of gifts under the big Christmas tree.

For weeks, toy donations had been hauled from Hyden in wagons, and women had been holding sewing bees to make clothing for babies and dolls.

All of Leslie County was invited to this Christmas dinner, and 500 showed up. Breckinridge was determined that every child would have candy and a gift. Each one was led to the tree to choose a present.

"This was terribly hard on the boys as they stood with dazzled eyes in front of balls, harmonicas, little red trucks. As for the girls, there was not one but wanted a doll and there weren't enough dolls to go around."

Every child had a toy, but some girls who wanted dolls had to settle for a make-believe one.

"The doll of one such little girl was a piece of old blanket, tied around the middle with a string, with a stone fastened at one end for a face. But she loved it, with that creative instinct older than recorded time, which springs up anew in every girl baby. Why must she needs mother something, with the first outreaching of her tiny hands …?

"When Christmas comes we understand a little less dimly. The Light of the World could only come to his own through a woman's body. Only a woman held the mysteries of his Advent and pondered them in her heart."

A group of Hyden schoolchildren sang *O Come, All Ye Faithful, O Little Town of Bethlehem* and *Silent Night*, and after a prayer Breckinridge dedicated a bronze plaque on the chimney to her two children, whose deaths—one at birth and the other at age 4—had caused her to turn to nursing.

The plaque, which reads, "To the glory of God and in memory of Breckie and Polly, Dedicated Christmas 1925," is still on the fireplace in the Big House, which now serves as a bed and breakfast and is listed on the National Register of Historic Places. It is also one of 30 National Historic Landmarks in Kentucky.

More than 20,000 births would be attended by Frontier Nursing Service midwives in Leslie, Clay and Perry counties in the decades after that first Christmas. And though Breckinridge died in 1965, her legacy to life continues through Frontier Nursing University in Hyden.

I wonder what Breckinridge and the little girl with the doll made with a blanket, a stone and a piece of string would think today of what has become of Christmas.

DECEMBER 2012

Gifts of time

Come back with me this Christmas season to a place in Kentucky where a young boy once sat on a log in a thicket of red cedars, watching and listening—but mostly listening—as snowflakes tumbled in peaceful profusion from a misty gray sky. The boy, who couldn't have been more than 12, had been to this place before, but never when snow was falling so softly upon the cedars.

The boy was me.

My ears were good back then. Not ringing as they are today. So the silence, broken only by the hushed percussion of snowflakes coming to rest upon one another, left with me a memory that has lasted all these years.

I didn't realize at the time that those few moments of winter solitude in God's snowscape on a hillside above a creek would never be duplicated. Though I tried to go back there later, when the snow fell again, there was never another time when I found nature in such perfect harmony: the wind so calm, the light a mellow haze upon the valley of canebrakes and fence rows that I loved, the snowflakes of the right design to produce a gentle rustling, as though a thousand tiny gifts were being unwrapped under the cedars.

How odd that among my trophy memories of Christmas seasons come and gone, the ones with no bells and whistles are my favorites.

These memories are Father Time's gifts to me as I grow older.

If I had left the cedar thicket that snowy day and followed the creek most of a mile downstream, I'd have come to an old stock barn, long since vanished, that held an even warmer memory of the season.

Late one afternoon, when I must have been about 5 years old and the snow was maybe ankle deep, I followed in my dad's tracks down to the barn when we walked through the fields to feed the cattle. The barn was a pretty good walk from our farmhouse, and by the time we got there, I told Dad that my toes were really cold.

He sat me down on a bale of hay, knelt on his knee in front of me, took off my boots and socks, rubbed my toes, looked a bit worried, then did something I would never have expected.

He opened his old coat, unbuttoned his shirt, cradled my cold feet in his callused hands, and drew them inside his shirt, then pressed them against his belly to warm.

In that little moment, maybe for the first time in my young life, I remember thinking, "Daddy must really love me a lot to put my cold feet against his belly."

My toes may have gotten cold again that afternoon, but my heart was warmed for life.

This Christmas, my wish for you and those you love is that Father Time has brought you enough warm memories to last long after this year's gifts are forgotten.

Merry Christmas.

DECEMBER 2013

Story time

My friend John Morrow was in a bit of a hurry. He had dropped off some keys to his daughter, Dena, a nurse at a local nursing home, and then had another stop to make.

As he passed an older man in a wheelchair, the patient asked, "Would you talk to me?"

"I sure will," said John. "What do you want to talk about?"

"Farming," the old man answered, without hesitation.

Somewhat taken aback—and suddenly aware that this conversation might last a while—John, a caring man, assured the old gentleman that he certainly would talk with him about farming, but that he was rushed at the moment and would be back.

A few days later, before John returned, his daughter told him that the old man had died. His mind was still good, she said, but in all the time he had been in the nursing home, she knew of no one who had come to visit and listen to the stories he wanted to share about farming.

John was deeply saddened. He truly had intended to get back, but did not realize that the old man's life would end so soon. On reflection, he recently told his Sunday school class, whatever he had to do that day could have waited.

Many of us may relate to John's story on some level, perhaps in the memory of a patient we have passed in a nursing home hallway while visiting a friend or relative, someone who offered a hopeful hello and a timid smile as we were leaving.

The face you remember might be that of an old veteran who had no family left, or of a mother whose children never came to visit, or of someone who had simply outlived everyone they knew. One woman I remember had been a writer for *Collier's* magazine during its glory years. I meant to return for an interview, but never got back.

I recalled, too, a lonely old gentleman who passed the time each day counting cars on the Norfolk Southern trains that rumbled past on the railroad near the nursing home. He had a click counter, and had carefully recorded each day's totals in a writing tablet.

Almost everyone has a story. One man who was nearing 100 had forgotten nearly everything, but his eyes brightened and a smile spread across his face when he shared sweet memories of the smartest dog he ever owned.

As I ponder my friend John's story and my own regrets, in the rush of last-minute shopping for gifts, it occurs to me that if we really want to do something nice for someone this Christmas, there must still be many residents of nearby nursing homes waiting for someone who wants to hear their stories.

It just may be that if we take time to listen, our most memorable gift this Christmas will be theirs.

DECEMBER 2014

Prayers and presents

In the gathering glow of Christmas present, a wondrous story of giving is unfolding in the mountains of Harlan County.

This Christmas, 61-year-old Michael Howard, a retired coal miner, will stuff pillows into his Santa suit for the 39th straight year and settle into a chair in the back of his white 2006 Ford pickup decorated with ribbons and Christmas lights and loaded with gifts.

Then he will begin handing out toys and candy for five or six nights through Christmas Eve to hundreds of children who live in the hills and hollows along the Poor Fork of the Cumberland River and beyond.

When one truck is empty, another load of presents from a trailing toy convoy will take its place, and then another, and another. Last Christmas, Howard, his wife, Barbara, their three children, and a happy cadre of helpers distributed 115 loads of new toys—about 3,000, all of them wrapped—and 3,500 bags of treats.

Wide-eyed youngsters wait in mountain yards for hours to see Santa's pickup appear.

"You just load them down with presents and treat bags. Some of them don't even go in the house, just sit right down there in the snow or on the ground and open their presents," Howard says. "On the way home on Christmas Eve,

I cry because I'm out of toys and have to quit."

Helpers are often moved to tears by the heartwarming scenes they encounter. Howard, who grew up poor in a family of 11 children, is known to return later to some homes, bringing shoes and clothing for families in need.

As news of his efforts spread via Steve Flairty's book, *Kentucky's Everyday Heroes,* and other media, Howard's 16- by 28-foot storage shed where he began storing and wrapping gifts grew to a 120-foot-long block structure that fills to capacity with thousands of mostly new toys well before December each year.

Volunteers from North Carolina, Tennessee, Mississippi, Ohio and other states show up to help. A Louisville woman brings a 20-foot-long truck loaded with new toys, and four people from a church in southern Mississippi arrived back in the summer with more than 1,000. Some of Howard's volunteers remember him giving them toys when they were children.

Howard shuns credit for the amazing success of the project, insisting it is the answer to daily prayers that he lifts to the Almighty on his knees in the woods on the mountain behind his home.

"I try to stay where he wants me. If the Lord wasn't in it, we couldn't do it," he says.

Howard also visits two Harlan nursing homes and the jail each week with words of encouragement and snacks bought with donations. And he has given 48 truckloads of toys for Christmas gifts to children elsewhere in Harlan County.

DECEMBER 2016

Not forgotten at Christmas

Christmas was a long time coming for Peggy Hubbard, but when it finally found her she began sharing its joy with hundreds of children in Lincoln County who were at risk of being forgotten at Christmas, as she once was.

Her alcoholic father abandoned her mother and their eight children when Peggy was too young to remember, and her mother died of cancer when Peggy was 4.

The last words she heard her mother say were, "Kids, be quiet, because Momma's very sick."

After her mother died a few hours later, Peggy thought for a long time that if they had only been quiet, their mother might have lived.

No one came forward to take the four boys and four girls, who were moved from their home in Floyd County to an orphanage in Virginia. The one time their father came to see them, one of Peggy's older brothers ran after the car, crying, as his father was leaving—and she remembers the home's superintendent making the other children watch as he switched the boy until his legs bled.

The children were eventually put out of the home due to a lack of funding for their care. One of Peggy's brothers hitchhiked back to eastern Kentucky to find someone to come get them.

So began life for a little girl from the mountains in the late 1940s. And it would not get much better for several years.

The children later lived by themselves in what had once been a chicken house, and where three of the children died—Peggy's little sister, it was believed, from malnutrition and complications from a rat bite on her toe while she was sleeping.

At age 13, Peggy managed to get to Lexington and was taken in by a family whose children she helped care for. She married while still in her early teens and moved with her husband, Donald, to Cincinnati, where they both worked and where she had her first Christmas.

The couple moved to Lincoln County in 1976 to care for Don's aging mother, and later established a successful hardware business. Then Peggy, a member of Inter-County Energy, started her own annual charity event, Winterfest, for Lincoln County children who might not have a Christmas.

Using much of her own money in the early years, and what donations that came her way, she bought truckloads of gifts for children in need who'd been identified only by age and gender.

Since the late 1980s, thousands of children have had gifts under a large Christmas tree, a Christmas dinner, treats and a visit with Santa.

A former Lincoln County Citizen of the Year, Peggy, 70, is now the caregiver for Don, who has a debilitating illness. But Winterfest continues under the supervision of community leaders, with generous donations from local businesses.

It is a legacy of giving from the heart of a woman who remembers what it was like to be forgotten at Christmas.

DECEMBER 2017

Christmas train

All too soon our bookmark moments of Christmases past are edged in poignant thoughts of loved ones no longer with us.

I suppose that is why many of us, each Christmas season, leaf through the pages of our memory books all the way to childhood—when the simple glow of lights on a tree, the toy section in a Christmas mail order catalog, or the magical spell of Christmas songs once lifted us to a place where only the mind of a child finds room to wander.

Esther Jo Long recalls a bookmark Christmas when she was about 5 years old—more than 75 Christmases past.

Her family lived in a two-story farmhouse in Shelby County beside what then was the Louisville & Nashville Railroad. Her father was a tobacco farmer; her mother a homemaker.

Esther Jo, the youngest, with four much older siblings, was often playing in the yard or "helping" her mother hang clothes on the line when trains passed. She waved to the engineer and to crewmen in the caboose who sometimes tossed a surprise to her from the train window: chewing gum, candy or a coloring book and crayons.

Once, when the train was stopped, the engineer—who had a long white beard like Santa Claus—got permission from Esther Jo's mother to let her board the big steam locomotive and blow the whistle. She still remembers the engineer's name: J.J. Allen, from Winchester.

In those lean, post-Depression years of the late 1930s, her father had little to show for his hard work on the farm, but Esther Jo remembers a happy home.

On a Christmas morning when deep snow covered the landscape, she stood in the window beside their Christmas tree, waiting to wave as the train rumbled past.

"When we heard the train coming down the track, Mom raised the window … and I remember how we could hear it slowing down, slowing down, and we wondered if something was wrong."

As the train slowed to a crawl, a conductor standing on the bottom step of a passenger coach gently placed a big box in the snow near the Morris's side yard.

"I get emotional every time I talk about it," Esther Jo says. "Of course I started jumping up and down, and screaming and carrying on, and daddy waded out in the snow and brought the box in."

Inside was a beautiful doll that looked about 2 feet tall, wearing a long dress and bonnet. The attached note read, "From your railroad friends."

Esther Jo would likely still have the cherished doll and note had not a fire destroyed the Morris home and nearly all their possessions, including the doll, a few years later.

But evergreen memories are fireproof.

Never a Christmas passes that the far-off echo of a train whistle doesn't warm Esther Jo's heart and call back the joy of that snowy morning when she was 5.

So sweet is the memory that she is still smiling.

DECEMBER 2018

Christmas tree

Somewhere beneath the tangled tinsel of a Christmas past lies hidden the story of the loneliest Christmas tree in Kentucky.

That's what I call the eastern red cedar standing all alone on a grassy ribbon of roadside along the eastbound lanes of the Bluegrass Parkway in Nelson County.

I first noticed it as a blur out the SUV window while passing at 70 miles an hour two or three summers ago.

Had I just seen a Christmas tree all by itself stirring in the midsummer breeze—strung with tinsel and ornaments—virtually in the middle of nowhere?

There was no time for a double take, and I was still about 2 1/2 miles from the U.S. Highway 31E exit near Bardstown. But I promised myself I'd give the tree a closer look if it was still there when I passed that way again.

So back in August on one of those rare, lazy, white-cloud-and-blue-sky-days when time itself seems at rest, I pulled to the shoulder and studied the tree for a while, then got out and walked over beside it. I guessed it to be between 15 and 20 feet tall and maybe 8 feet in diameter at the base.

Though not a very pretty cedar as live Christmas trees go, someone had dolled it up with half a dozen or more strands of red and silver tinsel and upward of 80 nice ornaments, counting several that had blown off and were on the ground. (You don't want to linger too long beside a busy highway, counting Christmas ornaments on a cedar tree in the middle of August.)

Some of the red, silver and blue ornaments were as large as a grapefruit and hanging as high as a tall person could reach. At least three solar lights were suspended from branches above the decorations.

There wasn't a building in sight; nothing but woodlands and a long grassy meadow beyond the right-of-way that fell gently away to a creek.

A clerk at the convenience store a few miles away said she was pretty sure she'd first noticed the tree at least five years ago, but maybe longer.

Who decorated it, and why? Perhaps someone overwhelmed with the Christmas spirit? Maybe someone whose car—loaded with Christmas decorations—broke down near the tree one Christmas Eve. Or a lovesick young man or woman whose sweetheart often passed the tree. We may never know.

And while the lonely old cedar may never see pretty packages under its tired branches and faded ornaments, there is wrapped in its shadow the simple gift of a Christmas memory for a homesick traveler who, in the blink of an eye, may be carried back to warm thoughts of a distant Christmas past before vanishing out of sight in the fast lane.

Merry Christmas to you—whoever you are—for decorating the loneliest Christmas tree in Kentucky. And Merry Christmas to all of you from *Kentucky Living*.

JUNE 2019

The rest of the story

You may be ready for summer, but I'm still tying up loose ends from last Christmas.

In December I wrote about what I called "the loneliest Christmas tree in Kentucky," an eastern red cedar bedecked with Christmas ornaments standing all alone on a grassy strip of right-of-way beside the eastbound lanes of the Bluegrass Parkway in Nelson County. I've been passing the tree for several years and wondering who decorated it and why.

Don Fulford of Perryville, Missouri, wrote to say that he's responsible.

In April 2008, while living in Elizabethtown, he took a job in Versailles and was driving 83 miles one-way each morning and evening.

"After several months of this drive I noticed a very lonely looking evergreen sitting all by itself at mile marker 18," Fulford says. "I couldn't figure out why they hadn't cut it down when they cleared the rest of the side of the road, and why it spoke to me each morning and night as I took that long, lonely drive."

He'd read an inspirational article called *The Trouble Tree* (author unknown), about handling stress by figuratively hanging one's troubles on a tree each evening and picking them up the next morning. So, when his wife handed him a box of old Christmas ornaments they found while cleaning the attic that summer, Fulford smiled and put them in his car. Then he began hanging a few on the lonesome cedar before daylight each morning.

"The tree was much smaller back then, and I could actually reach the top!"

Fulford says he hoped it would give others a smile, and perhaps great memories of Christmases gone by.

He thought the story would end there, but it didn't. Soon, others began hanging more ornaments on the tree, and even a small string of solar lights.

"I've since moved away, but still get texts from friends who smile when they see the tree," he writes. "I was always worried about getting in trouble, so I've never used my name—but hopefully the good law people of the state realize it was all done in the spirit of living and Christmas. Thank you again for the article."

DECEMBER 2020

A teacher's Christmas

Christmas was just around the corner and, despite hard times in the once-thriving Harlan County coal mining community of Wallins Creek, the first-graders in Judith Hensley's class at Wallins School were aglow with excitement.

Their Christmas tree was strung with decorations they had made or brought from home, their imaginations warmed with Christmas stories and songs of the season. It was the early 1980s. A sharp decline in coal production and slow recovery from a devastating flood some years earlier had dampened spirits in Wallins Creek, but not the evergreen enthusiasm of these first-graders.

Judith, a divorced mother, had been teaching only about four years, and remembers her students that year as a wonderful group of 25 children. Some of them reminded her of youngsters she had seen in the *Little House on the Prairie* or *The Waltons* television series.

Her budget was limited, but she made sure that every child in her class had treats and a small gift or two under the tree—maybe a coloring book and crayons, a small toy or jump rope, and often whatever school supplies they seemed to need.

While some students were naturally outgoing and the center of attention, the little boy who often caught Judith's eye rarely said much. His name was Roger.

"I could always look at him and tell what he was thinking or feeling. He just wore his heart in his eyes. He was such a sweet little guy. Tough as nails, but he had such a good heart."

Although gifts for the teacher were not expected, as the school's Christmas break drew near, some children gave Judith gifts, perhaps a piece of fruit, a pencil holder or other small item.

"The day Roger brought his present up to my desk—when no one else was around—he stood there at first and wouldn't say anything. He had his hand behind his back, and I said, 'What have you got there, Roger?'

"He looked at me, and I could tell there was a little bit of nervousness and that he was a little bit scared, but with a whole lot of love he brought his little hand out from behind his back and said, 'I brought you a present, teacher, and I wrapped it myself. I thought if you didn't have one of these, you might need it.'

"Well, the present was wrapped in a scrap of Christmas paper, and wrapped in black electrical tape. It was about an inch or an inch and a half long, and when I opened it up … it was a safety pin.

"That's still one of my all-time most precious Christmas gifts, ever.

"At that time, we weren't afraid to touch children, so I grabbed him and wrapped him up in a bear hug and hugged him with all my heart—and told him that was one of the best presents I ever got.

"Every time I retell the story I almost cry."

DECEMBER 2021

Gift of imagination

When many of us were kids, the arrival of a Christmas catalog in the mailbox about this time every year was the next best thing to Christmas morning.

Amazon was still only a great river in South America back then, and online retailing was hiding somewhere in uncharted cyberspace.

In the soft glow of Christmas tree lights, even toys in the catalog's dull sepia-tone pages took on a magical luster. And in the color pages, if we listened closely, we could almost hear the whistles of electric trains and the bang of cap pistols—or sobs from a doll called Tiny Tears. Her description said she cried, wet her diaper, closed her eyes at naptime and blew bubbles just like a real baby.

With a little Christmas music, a rich imagination and a Christmas catalog, we could lay claim to any toy by simply touching its picture with our peppermint-sticky fingers in those days. And if we closed our eyes, we could picture all the toys we would probably never have—under the tree in the shadows of the bubble-lights.

Some kids curled up in an easy chair to lose themselves in the pages of a Sears, Roebuck & Co. "Wish Book"; others preferred lying propped on their elbows near the tree.

There, perhaps between the nativity set on one side and lights and tinsel on the other, the religious and material spirits of Christmas peacefully co-existed in many homes. Local radio stations often broadcast the Christmas story, and most featured Santa reading letters from boys and girls asking for toys they'd likely seen in the catalog.

Toy trucks and bulldozers, guns, dolls and dollhouses, record players, pedal cars and bikes were popular. Santa was fond of Lincoln Logs, and of the View-Master, with special lenses through which some of us would first glimpse 3-D images of Old Faithful and Mount Rushmore.

Grown-ups leafing through the Sears Christmas catalog in 1954 found a number of black-and-white televisions, from a 17-inch table model priced at $117.95 to a deluxe 21-inch screen console for about $300. A special notice to customers explained that as the Christmas catalog went to press, color televisions, which were relatively new to the market, were three to four times more expensive than black-and-white sets, and that color televisions would be listed in the catalog when it became more practical to do so. "Right now," the notice said, "we feel that Silvertone black-and-white is your best TV buy."

Black-and-white sets were soon to be a thing of the past, and many Christmas catalogs would eventually go paperless or become much smaller. But one or two thin catalogs sometimes still show up in our mailbox about this time of year to remind me that, for many of us, one of the best gifts of our childhood was the gift of imagination.

DECEMBER 2022

Memories evergreen

Christmas present shares its glow with Christmases past each year in the Bracken County seat of Brooksville, where many families gather on the courthouse lawn to decorate Christmas trees in memory of loved ones.

Since the Bracken County Historical Society began placing memorial Christmas trees around the courthouse in 2014, society President Jan Fatka says what began with about 15 trees has grown to 100 in Brooksville (population, 654). Forty more trees are placed in nearby Augusta, the original county seat, which was moved to the more central location of Brooksville in 1839.

Trees are sold for $100 each, and though prices have increased over the years, there is a waiting list at both locations. The number of trees had to be limited due to a lack of space and lighting availability.

With help from the Bracken County High School FFA and other volunteers, the historical society places the trees, strings them with lights and posts signs indicating who sponsored each tree and in whose memory. Individuals are then invited to hang ornaments on the trees they have sponsored.

Heather Brumley, a teacher who lives in rural Milford, has sponsored three trees for several Christmases: one in memory of her paternal grandparents, one for her maternal grandparents and mother, and another for her late son.

One set of her grandparents had 11 children, so the family made picture ornaments for that tree. Her brother served in the military, and Heather decorates his tree with mostly red, white and blue ornaments.

"When you walk through, you can just kind of see the personality of a family in how they have represented those loved ones," Heather says.

Mary Ann Kearns, editor of the *Maysville Ledger Independent*, sponsors a tree in memory of the son she lost in 2009. One Christmas his tree was trimmed with his childhood favorite figures from *Star Wars*; another was decorated with an *Indiana Jones* theme.

"It's a happy tree, and a happy remembrance of him."

Judy Cooper, a longtime consumer-member of Blue Grass Energy and a historical society volunteer, sponsors a tree each year in memory of her late son, her husband, other family members and friends. "People who've moved away and don't have family here anymore still do trees," she says. "It's just a nice way to remember someone."

The Bracken County Historical Society often dedicates trees to members it has lost during the year, and last year to noted Kentucky writer Ed McClanahan, a native of Brooksville, who had just passed away.

Trees are bought from a local home improvement store, and lights are always turned on by the first Saturday in December and left on round-the-clock until after New Year's.

Out-of-towners often visit Brooksville to see the trees during December, and sometimes a dusting of snow adds a Christmas card effect to the nighttime scene of lights and memories among the evergreens.

ABOUT THE AUTHOR

As Byron Crawford tells it, his story doesn't begin on the Lincoln County farm where he was born in 1945, or with the 1960s high school field trip that led to his first radio broadcast, or even when he left WHAS-TV in 1979 to take the mantle of the coveted Kentucky Column at Louisville's *The Courier-Journal*.

Instead, the roots of Crawford's journey of more than 5,000 newspaper columns, television and radio reports, and the monthly dispatches appearing on the back page of *Kentucky Living* since 2011, can be found at his father's knee in rural Kentucky.

"I listened to a lot of great storytellers, friends of my Dad at the feed mill or at the stockyards, or in the tobacco barn, people who dropped by to visit," Crawford recalls. "And I would have to be quiet, and the other kids would, too. We would all have to listen."

The Kentucky Journalism Hall-of-Famer says hearing how those storytellers handled a story may have been the best education he ever received on how to present a story.

"They knew how to get you hooked at the beginning. They filled it with some details that were interesting and informative. And they usually tied it up in a bow at the end, where it had some meaning," Crawford says. "If it was a funny story, that's where the biggest laugh came. If it was a story that pulled at your heartstrings, then that ending would do it."

Crawford's secret ingredient is authenticity, says his longtime friend and fellow Kentucky writer, Ike Adams, best known for his newspaper column, Points East.

"There's just a blatant honesty," Adams says. "He can tell the story in real terms, really understandable terms without doing any embellishment or any alteration of the facts at all. He's got that level of detail and I think that's a very rare talent to be able to do that. Byron is Kentucky's truthteller."

Adams recalls some of the people profiled by Crawford over the years, among them a hubcap collector "someplace on 27 between Stanford and Pulaski County," a top-notch slingshot target shooter who would "throw cans up in the air and the guy could bust them," and a mushroom hunter who astounded Crawford with his ability.

"I think he's a mirror for those of us who have a pride similar to his," Adams says with a smile. "Byron is proud of rural Kentucky, and it just shows."

The only child of Delbert and Lucille Crawford, Byron Garrison Crawford grew up on the family farm halfway down a 2-mile-long, dead-end gravel road near Hanging Fork Creek, adjacent to the farms of his uncle and great-aunt. Neighbors would drop by unannounced to visit.

"We raised tobacco, milked cows, had a few cattle, raised some corn, and I had the run of all of that territory," Crawford recalls. "Fences didn't mean much to us in those days."

Looking out the window of his high school, the young Byron would daydream about exploring Kentucky, envisioning a career in forestry.

"I can remember the desk. I remember the window in the school. We were on the second floor. I can remember when everybody else was supposed to be working, and I was, too," Crawford chuckles. "I had my eye on this fence line of woodlands off in the distance dreaming about maybe what was in there and wishing that I could get in there.

"I just roamed through the creeks and streams and woods and briar patches from daylight to dark sometimes, and I think it gave my imagination a real chance to develop."

That inborn curiosity turned out to be a natural fit for a gifted writer who says he has learned something from almost all of his interviews.

"I always wondered what was the little story within the big story," Crawford explains. "That was kind of what I wanted to build my career around."

His career includes radio news reporting for both WAKY and WHAS in Louisville and smaller radio stations in Danville and Richmond. While working in the late 1960s at WCKY in Cincinnati, Crawford would also serve as a disc jockey and television anchor with an Armed Forces Network Reserve unit.

But it was his work as a WHAS-TV feature reporter that would set the course for the rest of his career: nearly three decades of columns in *The Courier-Journal* and statewide television exposure on Kentucky Educational Television's *Kentucky Life* program.

Eric Crawford, the oldest of Byron and Jackie Crawford's four children, is now a sports reporter for WDRB-TV in Louisville. Eric, who also wrote for *The Courier-Journal*, says his father is among the last in a distinguished line of statewide newspaper columnists.

"He's interested in things and wrote about things that may or may not have a place in mainstream media anymore," Eric says. "So, he occupies a very important place in my view of telling the stories of this state from border to border, to people in the cities that don't always hear those stories."

In 2009, Crawford's byline first appeared in *Kentucky Living* magazine—an article about heroes of Kentucky's electric cooperatives.

When his friend, legendary columnist David Dick, died one year later, Byron humbly accepted his latest assignment—the back-page column of *Kentucky Living* that Dick had written for 21 years.

"I've tried to keep my writing on that back page in the vein that I thought David would appreciate," Crawford says.

Dick's widow and fellow writer, Lalie Dick, agrees.

"The wonderful thing about Byron is that he has an innate sense about being able to listen," Dick says. "He listens to people. And, now when people are talking over one another all the time, by phones or cells or whatever, he makes people slow down. His is a calming manner of writing that makes you want to curl up with a good book or just learn to sit there and listen to him."

The late Jackie Crawford, Byron's high school sweetheart and wife of 56 years, said in a 2017 interview that he rejected many offers to leave Kentucky.

"He's always felt an affinity for the people here," she said. "He's loved all the people that he did stories on and he remembers them after all these years."

To his legions of *Kentucky Living* fans whose letters and emails praise past columns and submit ideas for future ones, Crawford says he finds simple truths and profound meaning in the real-life stories of Kentuckians.

"I want this back page to be the people's chance to tell their stories," Crawford says, smiling. "I'm just a guy who takes down the notes."

Written by Joe Arnold, vice president of strategic communications at Kentucky Electric Cooperatives; originally published in the August 2018 edition of Kentucky Living.